SCHOOL DAZE

ASHANTÉ

ISBN: 978-0-578-46432-9

CONTENTS

FOREWORD

Ashanté is an amazingly deep, loving, and complex woman with a strong sense of fairness and inner strength that has propelled her forward in her life in a way that is very different than people might have expected. Ashanté grew up on the South Side of Chicago. The South Side is notorious for its poverty, violence, and presence of street gangs and drugs. It is arguably the roughest part of all of Chicago. Many children growing up in Chicago, unfortunately never get the opportunity to realize, or even know, their potential. I should know; I was a high school principal in Englewood and Ashanté's principal at TEAM Englewood Community Academy High School, where she attended all four years and received her high school diploma.

School Daze is a must-read for anyone who wonders about the human capacity to achieve against all odds. This is the life and struggles of an inner-city youth who is able to do the work required to emerge from her extremely tough shell to transform into who she always was, but that even she did not know.

As the founding principal of TEAM Englewood, our mission was to help Englewood students realize their potential by surrounding them with amazing staff and teachers, high expectations, and a lot of patience and love. Ashanté and her twin brother Allanté, came to the school and made their presence known immediately. They were smart and well known. They would crack jokes and get everyone riled up, and it was difficult to get them to focus on their academics. Still, they came in with the highest test scores of anyone in their class.

Ashanté's extreme sense of fairness kept her balanced. If she got into trouble and knew she deserved it, she would accept it without issue. But, if she got into trouble and she didn't think she deserved it, things got out of hand quickly. She would talk back to teachers, leave without permission—showing she was in charge of her life and would do what she wanted. Many teachers felt exasperated, not knowing how to handle Ashanté in their classrooms. They referred her to my office, frequently.

Ashanté would arrive in my office, usually accompanied by a flustered security officer who would tell me what Ashanté did. She would look at me and sit down, I would excuse the security officer, and we would talk. I'd ask her—what happened? And she would tell me. In most cases, I was able to point out to her where she went wrong, and how she could have handled the situation better. In other cases, I felt she was totally right and we still talked about how she could have handled it better. Because she had developed a reputation, she sometimes was unfairly, blamed for things that happened in class. What I loved about talking with Ashanté, is how well she listened to my advice and counsel. I had earned her trust. She knew I would listen and had her best interest at heart, and so this afforded me the ability to talk to her directly and honestly. Often times, after we dealt with the situation at hand, we'd talk about other things happening in her life. I got a real glimpse of how difficult it was for Ashanté to code-switch; to act one way out in the streets, and to turn off the aggressiveness, distrust, and anger so she could truly concentrate in school. This was something that most of my students dealt with, and that was our biggest challenge—to help students slowly peel off the layers so they could actually trust us enough to believe in their potential. In my eyes, this battle mattered most. If we could get through to our students, enough to have them trust us and to release their protective shield to acknowledge their potential, then we had a shot with them.

Over Ashanté's four years, everyone knew if she was having a bad day—take her to Ms. Korellis. She and I developed a special bond where I could just look at her and she would know what I expected of her. She could come to my office and take a deep breath. I often thought *how do I save this girl from herself?* In reality, she saved herself.

In the years since high school, Ashanté has found a way to transform her life in every aspect. She joined the military because she knew she needed to leave Chicago, and she felt the discipline of the military would help her focus her life. I was so proud of her for making that decision, and I knew that once Ashanté changed her environment and got to see the world, the real Ashanté would emerge. The Ashanté *I* got to know. But even I couldn't have imagined the depth and breadth of her transformation, while remaining true to her very core.

School Daze is a beautifully written story of Ashanté's experiences, about how a girl from Chicago was able to save herself from a life expected for her, by some, but was never in her heart. She was able to do the work to find out who she really is and let that person come to life. Ashanté's story is unique because it is hers, and we are able to see how she overcame so many obstacles to live her best life. Her story gives hope to so many young people, who are struggling right now, in the same ways she was. It also will inspire anyone, whether you've struggled in the same manner or not, to take that seed that is hidden in your heart and let it bloom.

Peggy Korellis, Ed.D.
    Founding Principal of TEAM Englewood
    Chicago, IL

BORN TO BE

AS A KID, it did not take much to catch my eye. Everything I came across was intriguing to me in some way or another. My mother raised my five siblings and me in such open-minded manner. She always instilled in us two things: to never say never and not to say what we can't do, because anything is possible. The word "can't" weighed on the same scale as cussing in our household. My oldest brother, Anthony, taught me to rise above any struggles. My oldest sister, Artika, taught me to keep faith and gratitude, if nothing else. My twin brother, Allanté, showed me how to think for myself and ask questions when in doubt. My baby sister, Arikka, often reminded me to be a go-getter because she was always looking up to me. For these reasons, my curiosity sparked at an early age. From knowledge, to sports. And even the homeless people I passed by on a daily basis. My siblings and I used to walk to the CTA bus stop early mornings for school, when we lived in the city. I remember the group of men and women that rested under the Cottage Grove bus stop with comforters, pillows, and shopping buggies filled with canned goods and collectibles. Had we not been running late, we made it our business to interact. Often, I didn't start to say anything. I just posted up on their bus stop with the anticipation of a kid watching a stranger unravel candy, hoping they'll offer some. Anthony was the most social of us all, and the most hilarious. His humor was a perfect segue into my engagement. It didn't take long for the men and women to initiate a conversation. Typically, their end goal was to receive spare change- they were always sure to ask. Most days, all I had to offer were jokes and giggles. Still, they never fail short in dialogue. Some of them were familiar drug addicts in the neighborhood, who were overly persistent in their efforts. There were times I tried to disguise myself, so that I didn't have to deal with explaining why, as kid, I couldn't afford to support them. Still, most of them were full of wisdom, and laughter. I can't say for sure, how it's possible for people as wise as those good people to end up in such unfortunate situations, but they were content with life. That was most intriguing to me.

When I returned home from school, things operated differently. My siblings and I didn't always return together. We made sure we were on the same page in terms of what time my mama came in from work and what time we should be home so that we can get our chores done and homework started. As I unloaded the bus, the bus stop population had scattered. I made my way through the neighborhood, and read the same signs posted in the windows of the Social Security office and other official buildings, since probably before I were born. Some days I'd go straight home. Other days, I'd detour to the basketball court and watch the fellas-as often times, my cousin Dominique as the only girl hooper- play. Some of the old men who had been in the community long before myself, would stroll around the court as they collected plastic bottles and cans. I eagerly waited for them to get started at their storytelling of what the old days were like. They always had a few to tell. Like Curious George, I grew a rush for learning more.

Strangely, though, I've never been much of a television kid. There are some movies and shows I've seen maybe five or six times and have yet to absorb the contextual meaning. I was always very much a daydreamer.

Music, on the other hand, takes me away. On days I came home from school feeling anxious, due to conflicts with my peers I would blast music from my brothers' stereo or plug my mp3 headphones in and bury my head underneath my pillow. When I received academic achievements or any other good news, I had similar tactics. I'd twirl around the house happily to some of my favorite jams. Music has always been a way of life for me. I have a mental playlist of hundreds of songs that deeply resonate. From joyful to pitiful.

I never knew what I wanted to be when I grew up. In my heart and only the back of my mind, a gymnast always lingered. I never spoke on it, though. It simply didn't seem likely. There were no gymnasts playing around the neighborhood. Nor were there any known gymnasiums that offered that type of coaching- not that I knew, or even ever heard of. I always pondered when asked the question- What do you want to be when you grow up? I thoroughly enjoy helping others in just about any way possible, but still really had no desire to be anything or anyone for that matter. I used to think that was a bad thing, and eventually, I tagged myself as a future doctor. I found it necessary to live up to the modern-day expectations of institutionalists that look at you crazy if your dreams didn't align with some sort of hierarchy education. Every day, now, it is clear that I still have no desire to be anyone or anything. I crave simply to be.

━━

"Maybe the journey isn't about becoming anything. Maybe it's about unbecoming everything that isn't really you so that you can be who you were meant to be in the first place." -Unknown

━━

EARLY LAST YEAR, I was on the run from life. In a literal sense.

With just a few personal items, I drove for three days from Texas to Oakland, California. I was in search of answers to questions I didn't even quite know how to articulate. I spent all of my days in California journaling, meditating, and watching the lake waters flow effortlessly.

One Monday afternoon, I got in my car and drove to Emeryville. That's where the closest Panera Bread was located. I didn't know of any other places to get a decent plant-based meal. While at Panera, I took notice of their armed Black female security guard. I couldn't help but wonder why was the armed officer necessary. The restaurant filled with middle-class corporate employees. I ordered my food at the kiosk and sat at the table near the guard's post. Before a server brought my food out, I inquired. The security guard told me stories of the criminal activities that had been taking place over the last months. She mentioned that most of the suspects were identified as low-class minorities. As she carried on about the car break-ins, I scanned the restaurant, and observed the middle-class corporate workers. Many in their business suits or skirts and heels, as they surfed the web on their laptops. None of them seemed to be worried. I was confident the "takers" didn't want anything from my Hyundai Elantra. However, I hit my alarm again to be certain my doors locked. I got a bit nervous when I asked the guard, what she would do if she witnessed an act of theft by one of "minorities". She replied that she would "do her job," with an explicit look of earnestness. I feared for her.

When I finished my food, I hung around for twenty more minutes before I headed back to Lake Merritt. I got in the car, turned on a Tupac playlist, and cruised down the street in my four-door sedan. The vibes sparkled throughout the city. As I pulled up to the light on 12th Street, to my left was this woman with a gorgeously distinctive face structure and a blonde haircut that complimented her brown skin-tone. I was already grooving to the music, when my smile doubled in size as we caught eye contact.

I nodded my head and mouthed, "Your hair is beautiful."

She received my energy and rolled down her window. I reciprocated her action and asked her where she gets her hair done. I had just cut my hair off completely a few weeks before arriving in Oakland, and Lord knows I needed a credible stylist. The light changed just as she began to give me the name and directions to the shop. Cars honked their horns. The woman signaled for me to go ahead, and that she would follow. We parked, got out the car to exchange information, and winded up spending our entire day together down at the boat dock. We sipped some wine and discussed everything from the cost of living to business ventures and degrees. The girl's aura was vibrant and at only twenty-eight years old, she had a ton going for herself. We vowed to keep in touch and even communicated occasionally until I broke my phone at a fitness session.

BK Roots was the fitness studio where I decided to get a membership. I had dropped in at several yoga sessions throughout the city, and BK had the best fit. After a session there, I felt centered and rejuvenated. The yoga class prompted me to try out other classes offered there. I fell in love with Muy Thai. I began to attend Muy Thai classes every Tuesday, Thursday, and Sunday. My first Sunday class was when I broke my phone. I remembered there was a phone store just two blocks over from where I always parked, over at Lake Merritt. Only thing was, I couldn't figure out how to get back to that area. I decided to explore the neighborhood.

Many families had set up tents on the streets as their residency. Along with the tents, some of them even had couches and other furniture. There were entire "complex-like" set-ups that consisted of rows of tents occupied by different families. This occurred throughout the city. I planned to talk to some of them had I got close enough. I wanted to understand how the cost of living became so unmanageable. More so, at that moment, I needed to ask if they knew where the nearest phone store was located. I held off on bothering them with any of my questions, though. I preferred to respect their space. I walked a few blocks toward a busy street and ended up on Broadway. My stomach rumbled just as I looked up and saw Souley Vegan. Souley Vegan is a Black-Owned (POC as they call it in Oakland) vegan restaurant centered on Louisiana creole-style dishes and good music. The universe had remembered how hungry I was. I opted to dine in. The food was so delicious that I did not want to toss any of it. I overate and could have slept there in the restaurant's booth. Souley Vegan became a part of my Sunday routine. The soulful atmosphere was uplifting. I ate there every week until I left California.

I strolled back to my car, satisfyingly fatigued. I was able to get directions to the nearest phone store. I got my phone repaired and headed back to my temporary home, Lake Merritt.

After three months of isolation from the world, I sat on the dewy, summer green grass of Lake Merritt. I flipped through the pages of my journals when, those same questions I had traveled to California with, breezed through my mind. I grew weary as I expected some answers to surface. I read and reread what had come through me by way of pen meeting pad. My attention wandered to a time before any of this was possible. A light of cognizance shined on the fact that I had graduated high school well educated, but knew nothing at all. Certainly not who I was. Before any logic could connect myself to any bit of information imaginable, there was a voice inside of me itching for release.

I got on the road and headed back to Texas with the two three-subject notebooks filled with words. As I reflected on those entries, I had much more to value. I was able to realize that much of who I am is a direct reflection of many of the ordeals I experienced and adversities I witnessed at the schools I attended and in the neighborhoods, I lived. I went from deemed academically distinguished in my Chicago neighborhood school to transferring to a school that mainly served white middle to upper-class students, where my mama was told I didn't measure up to the reading level of my peers. That put my self-esteem on a slippery slope. My closest girlfriend left a quadriplegic after she was shot-down on the corner by where I lived. Or having to reroute my way home from school because coroners and authorities occupied my neighborhood streets, and to find that a close friend's body had been laying lifeless for over seven hours. It drained me of enthuse.

There are people with Post-Traumatic Stress Disorder that have never even been to Iraq or Afghanistan.

For me, writing has been the most therapeutic and has freed me from the mental torment of my lived experiences. My motivation is liberation. I pray that my story will shine light on the beauty of yours. This is my story.

CHAPTER ONE

JUST THE WAY IT IS

SEEMS THERE AIN'T BEEN MANY GOOD TIMES SINCE THE demolition of Cabrini Green. Cabrini Green was just one of the many housing projects in Chicago. They were to provide families of lower income- Black families- with affordable housing back in the 1930's. Many saw the projects to be the best housing you could get for the money if you were African American. Between Cabrini Green and the Robert Taylor Homes, where my mother and her nine siblings were raised, I heard a boatload of stories from their generations. Back in 1995, after lack of proper mainte- nance, the buildings had begun to deteriorate. The city had made plans to demolish the complex because it was symbolic for gangs, and other social ills like drugs and shoot- ings. Amongst the demolition plans, were other complexes to include the Ida B. Wells. The Ida B. Wells were located in the Oakland neighborhood on the Southside, opposed to Cabrini Green on the north. When the Ida B Wells project were first to undergo development, in 1939, the Oakland neighborhood was predominantly white. There was some protest about the project for African Americans. Many of the whites began to migrate elsewhere when they got notice the project would continue. The project housing consisted of row houses, mid and high-rise buildings, and a city park.

This is where most of my dad's side of family resided. I remember going to my cousin's apartments and having the time of my life each visit because we felt safe to run around the community carefree. Outside, we played Double Dutch, Hide n Seek, and Hop Scotch. Ice cream trucks came through and my dad bought ice cream for all of the kids that were around. There were candy stores that stayed open until late night. My dad often took us on candy store runs. Although my twin and I choices were limited to snacks like, chips and pickles, and fruit drinks, I appreciated those candy houses. We bundled up in our big coats, hats, scarves, and gloves. Chicago weather is complicated. We had snow on the ground with sunshine and clear skies. Fifty degrees in March was good play weather for us. The minute we got outside my dad chased us around the row houses. One by one, two by two's, all of us were playfully dunked in the snow. It was fun. When we recovered, my twin brother, cousins, and I made snow angels that glistened when the city streetlights came on. The Wells seemed like the ideal place to live.

MY MAMA HAD other plans for her family. She moved my siblings and me to Memphis with hopes of better living. I remember she had a job opportunity out in Memphis. My auntie, Phyllis, lived out there already. Auntie Phyllis was married and lived out of town with her husband and kids for some years before she moved back to Chicago. Auntie Phyllis stayed out the family loop so much that when she came around all she had was good home-cooked meals, and stories-whether they were real, over exaggerated or completely made up- to connect with the family. Growing up, I clung to Auntie Phyllis. Mostly because, I spent many days with her as a baby. Later in my life, I loved that she always gave me money to do chores around her house and she would let me help her in the kitchen. I enjoyed cooking. When we moved to Memphis, Auntie Phyllis used to babysit my siblings and me while my mama worked. Auntie Phyllis often reminded me of how I got my nickname, "Missy". She shared stories of how at just four months, I was flipping and turning out of my car seat. She said I would go from watching television to crawling with my car seat on my back. Meanwhile, my twin brother tuned in to the television, unbothered. I was tickled each time I heard the story of "Little Miss Missy".

After a few weeks of settlement into our new apartment in Memphis, we visited Chicago to get the remainder of our belongings. My mama's plan was to visit our family, secure our things, then get back on the road. As we prepared to head out, though, I hugged my grandma's ankles as if I was pair of ted hose. I cried, begged, and pleaded for my grandma to permit me to stay in Chicago. My grandma was from the Black Belt of the South, well poised in an abundance of love and pearls of wisdom. She told my mama to let my twin brother and I stay in Chicago. After contacting my dad, my mama agreed that we would. My dad filled with joy when he learned we would be staying with him. He picked us up from my Grandma's house. My twin brother and I were the happiest kids in the world. We hung out with my dad every day. He took us to carnivals, playhouses, and photo shoots. We even got to visit our cousins in the Ida B. Wells again, more often. Every day by nightfall, my dad would bathe us, read us bedtime stories, and tuck us into bed. It was close to anything that my dad would do for us— except allow us to eat candy. Before he stopped at a store for candy, he would pull over and buy whole seeded-water-melons from farmers that set up shop along the side of the road on Stony Island or down 63rd St.

One warm spring day, my dad took us out for fun. We went to a playhouse. He rolled around on the floor with us like a big kid. We ate food until our stomachs bloated. When we left the playhouse, Allante and I were exhausted. We slept in the car. My dad drove us to my Grandma's house for her to babysit us while he took care of business. I was happy to see my grandma. I grew happier when I saw my auntie, Lillie, was visiting too. Auntie Lillie was the third oldest of my mama's siblings. She had a norm of keeping a purse filled with candy, for us kids. She served in the United States Army, and had quite a different perspective of life. Auntie Lillie was open-minded and reserved, with a tranquil aura. Nothing ever seemed to bother her. When we saw Auntie Lillie, she embraced us and gave us a hand full of Tootsie Roll candy pieces. I put my candy in my pocket and went to jump in bed with my grandma to finish my nap time. When I woke up, I remembered my candy and went to town. When my dad returned to pick us up, he saw me chewing the candy. My dad took me into my grandma's bathroom and thumped me on my forehead. Then made me spit it out inside a napkin to trash it. That was the closest I had ever gotten to a "whooping". My feelings were crushed. As I began to cry, he went on to explain the harmful effects of candy. At four-years-old, I could care less but my dad's explanation buttered me up. The mere knowing of what I did wrong satisfied my emotions. My dad then gave me a fruit alternative and his warm hug made me forget all about the candy.

When we got back to my dad's place, he gave my twin brother and I a bath. He then put us on our pajamas and tucked us in bed, as usual. My dad planted a kiss on my forehead before leaving the room. His tender kiss soothed me sound asleep. The sound of his voice awakened me. I heard Auntie Lorraine, and my dad arguing. Auntie Lorraine was the only girl out of my father's siblings. She was strong-willed and had three kids of her own. Auntie Lorraine kids were all close to my age range. Actually, I'm not sure if my dad and auntie were arguing or not but they weren't very quiet. I remember the apartment door opened and closed shortly after their exchange of words. I went back to sleep.

I was shaken out of my sleep. I rubbed my eyes and whimpered, "I'm sleepy."

"Come on baby we gotta go" my auntie explained as she put my gym shoes on the wrong feet.

"Ouch! It hurt." I felt disoriented. It was as if I was sleep walking. Auntie Lorraine fixed my shoes and stayed busy as she multitasked to get the other kids dressed. She didn't pay me much of any mind.

I whined more, "These are pajamas."

My auntie's facial expressions and inattentiveness said she was exhausted. I didn't understand why my auntie was taking me outside before sunrise in pajamas and sneakers. We left out the house and loaded up in the car. I woke up, unwillingly, when the night wind swept across my face. In the car, the vibe was immensely melancholy. The stillness and awkward silence made it easy for me to fall back asleep. When I woke up, we were at my grandma's doorstep. We waited a couple minutes for someone to buzz. We hadn't

been there long before the apartment flooded with tears. I
learned that my father was shot and killed. I don't
remember crying. Even at the funeral. I was paralyzed with
fear.

━━━

Wadsworth

━━━

COLORED WITH CRAYONS OF SUNLIGHT, my
mama invariably emphasized the importance of health and
hygiene. Matching my siblings and me to a tee was practically necessary to her, too. Fashion and coordinating had
been one of her niches since before I was born. Old Navy
was one of her favorite places to shop for some years,
primarily because they were a one-stop shop for toddlers,
teenagers, and adult clothes. As often as possible, she would
dress all five of her kids alike, even when that meant the
girls wore boy-like gear. My mama never failed at making
sure we were well kept. I recall how every night my mama
laid out clean socks and underwear for us. My siblings and I
took turns showering while she cooked dinner. Most times, I
showered last to save some hot water for everybody else. I
had a habit of taking long. I used my shower time to pose
and play in the mirror and often forgot I had the shower
water running. And that I was supposed to be washing up.
Until my mother came knocking on the door for me to get
out of the bathroom.

Fall of 1999, I was just beginning my school years. I was
excited to start. My family had moved back to Chicago from
Memphis after my father was gunned-down in the city we

sometimes hate to love. My mother took pride in her roots but never fail short of acknowledging it wasn't always the best place to raise a family. Early on, she made my five siblings and me aware of the broken systems of society. She informed us how, as a young, Black, single-mother of five kids (at the time) it was not always easy to exceed the stigmas placed upon her. She warned us that things would not be much different for us, in terms of stigmas deposited. My mother was blessed in her abilities to adapt to change. She was always secure with God's Will. More than anything, she reminded my siblings and me that we are more than the stereotypes placed upon us as Black girls and boys from the hood. She had already lived a life for the survival of the fittest and didn't want for us to have to endure the same agony. My mama kept it utterly real with us about our community and stayed on us about our education. To her, education was a sure means of escaping the ghetto.

ON THE FIRST day of school, I walked into Kindergarten sporting my pink cheetah print vest; Allante had a similar vest with army fatigue print. Each of us had the backpack to match our vests; filled with color-assorted folders, freshly sharpened pencils, erasers, Elmer's glue and any other supplies my mama felt was essential to tackle our first year of elementary school. Just under my vest, I wore a white collared shirt tucked inside my navy school skort. My tights were streak-less, folded underneath my toes inside those spick and span dress shoes I hated wearing. My barrettes, reflecting my uniform colors, dangled from the two strand twists of my slick as cat-licked ponytails.

Waking up early to be sure everyone was nice and spiffy

was helpful, but being tidy didn't always come with good connotation. Bound with my lack of "social skills" it wasn't favorable amongst many of my peers. Some of my classmates assumed I was uppity and that made me bashful. I socialized with a few people, mostly those that sat at my table. Even then, I remember it would take them to forget toreturn my stuff, on several occasions for dialogue to be initiated. I simply wasn't good at starting a conversation nor continuing one for that matter. I hated small talk.

Some of my classmates admired the effort my mama put into my appearance. I got compliments all the time, but those compliments came along with ugly stares or nasty sidebar dialogue. When you're younger you think you could stand right behind a person in a single file line, look over your shoulder to whisper, and the person in front of you wouldn't hear it. Kayla Givens made it regular scheduled programming, whenever we got in line to go somewhere.

One day of many, she whispered, "she think she's the prettiest girl in the school that's why she don't talk to us."

"No, I don't" I looked back and rebutted.

Kayla rolled her eyes, "Nobody's talking to you!"

"But you're talking about me and I heard you so I'm gonna defend myself." I cut my eyes at her and walked off. It was my turn to enter the bathroom. I went to place toilet paper on the toilet seat just how my mama taught me to use public restrooms. As I unbuttoned my pants and sat down, tears began to fall. I was angry. Kayla always carried on about how I thought I was prettier than she was. I didn't get it. I barely talked. Though I never portrayed that "uppity" image, looking back, I couldn't blame her for feeling belittled. After all, it wasn't fair that someone always got to do things before her because their name comes before hers alphabetically. Or since she's much taller she has to stand behind me in the lunch line. It wasn't my fault either though. The problem we had was, five and six-year-olds couldn't quite whisper. I heard everything she ever said, even if she intended for me not to. Most times, I acted as if I didn't though. Instead, I shrunk myself and refrained from talking to anybody. On the good side, I still let them borrow my supplies all the time.

Feeling like an outcast, I began to reach. I made several attempts at "normalization" as my teacher once referred to it as. I remember I wanted so badly to work alone and she told me I needed to act more normal and participate like the other kids. I expanded conversation with Carmisha and Camera beyond our classroom table. I loaned out my supplies on more than enough occasions, which ultimately led to me getting in trouble at home. My mama used to restock our supplies throughout the school year but not everyone's parents did the same. If I had supplies to offer, I didn't mind sharing. Partly because I was raised to be generous and partly because I didn't want any backlash from my peers. Kids being kids often forgot to return my stuff. My mama had warned me one too many times about being more responsible with my supplies.

In retrospect, Carmisha and Camera were my girls. We played together at recess and even sat together at lunch many days. I liked them because they both had delightful personalities. They were very pretty on the inside and outside. Carmisha was more companionable than Camera and I. She had a medium caramel complexion with a natural, satin glow. One time a teacher asked her if she had on makeup. I thought it was a silly question for a teacher to ask a kid but the question wasn't taken offensively. Afterall, Carmisha's mother did used to coat her lips in red lipstick some days. Carmisha wore a vest and book bag identical to mine. I thought that made her even cooler. She always wore pretty button-up blouses and skirts with no tights; just ruffled socks and gym shoes. Camera was tall, pretty, had a milk chocolate complexion, and lovely hair that flowed over her shoulders. She was plain Jane, wearing a (gray or blue) cardigan, white polo and navy pants every day. There was so much beauty voiced in her simplicity. She usually wore tights underneath her pants, and big, black, bubble-shaped dress shoes, except for the days we had gym.

That particular day was, in fact, a gym day. Camera had left her sneakers at home. When the Physical Education teacher called roll and checked that we all had on proper gym uniform, she directed Camera to sit on the bench. Camera received no participation points for the day.

I was nearly in the same boat. After lunch, I jetted to the coat closet in our classroom to get my gym shoes. They were nowhere to be found. I knew my mama had put them in my book bag. After dumping everything out and finding a Nokia cell phone in the small pocket where my pencil box belonged, I realized I was at the wrong coat hook. I replaced everything in a hurry, went to my book bag, grabbed my shoes, and ran back to the gym.

Outside of the classroom or cafeteria, it was normal to catch me in my own world some days. However, today I wanted to play with Carmisha. Obviously, to talk about how cool it must be to have a cell phone already. Everybody had already scattered though. Carmisha played jump rope with her friends who were from another class, and Camera had a friend on the bench with her who she played hand games with like, "Shame-shame-shame" and "Ms. Mary Mack." I grabbed a single rope and jumped until my shoes unlaced themselves.

That is about the only thing that could've halted this

energizer bunny. Just as I sat my rope down to retie my
shoes Kayla went for the grab. Since I was already floor
level, I was able to retain the rope maybe just a millisecond
before her. She still caught the tail, which led us to a game
of tug-a-war. I could take a few meaningless words intended
to shut me down, but I wasn't about to let her take my rope.
My adrenaline began to rush as if I was just a dash from the
finish line with one runner in front of me. Kayla was much
bigger than I was, in height and weight. Yet each time she
pulled, my feet shuffled reluctantly, and I pulled right back,
and regained stability. All the while bargaining, "This mine,
get your own." She said nothing. Although the jump rope
belonged to neither of us, I did not feel compelled to give
her a turn right then. Barely hanging in there, I began to
gasp for air as she yanked me back and forth. Once I felt like
I reached full exhaustion, I maintained a loosening grip.
Instead of letting go, I let her yank me once more without
resistance and clenched her arm, which forced her to
release.

It didn't necessarily make me feel good or bad. At least
not until I saw the mark I had left. At first glance, it looked
as if someone had taken an old Coca Cola glass bottle cap,
pressed it into her arm, and then twisted it. There was a
pattern of dents enclosed by redness and broken skin. I sat
on the bench with a situated "ouch" facial expression as if I
felt her pain. I was shocked there was that much force in
me. Kayla and I had to stay at the gym to explain what
happened to our gym teacher so she could write up a report.
The rest of our class quietly headed back to the classroom in
a single-file line. The school day was ending. When I got
back to the classroom, Carmisha was crying. I figured she
felt bad for me. I told her I was okay. I understood what had
just happened, but I hadn't processed it emotionally.

Camera explained that somebody had actually stolen from Carmisha's stuff and that's why she was crying.

"What did they take?" I asked.

Camera replied, "She won't say"

Our teacher sent us to the coat closet to get our belongings.

Still curious, I asked "Carmisha what are you missing?"

"My phone" she sighed.

"Wait. I saw it just before gym class. I dumped your book bag thinking it was mine, when I came to look for my gym shoes."

"Fa'real? Girl my mama gone kill me," she whined.

"Yea fa'real, I put it back though. Right here where I found it," I explained.

I unzipped her side pocket, and her phone was there. That's certainly not the pencil pouch she knew she had placed it in though. She didn't care as long as she found it. She hugged me as tight as she did her mama every day when she came to pick her up, and with a smile just as big. She went to tell the teacher she had found her phone.

By the end of the day, not only did I get suspended pending parent-teacher conference for this incident, but I was also in trouble for touching another student's belongings-- stealing as it was referenced. All I know is that when my mama yelled at me about fighting in school, the lost phone story also surfaced. I wasn't the day saver, either. The teacher saw the term "stealing" as a fit label for what occurred.

Instinctively, I went into fight or flight mode when my mother talked to me about it. I attempted to argue both cases but didn't get far when I grew too frustrated. I felt hopeless in my efforts and let live whatever the teacher told my mama. To make matters worse, my mother was apprehended during the parent conference for my fight in gym class. Look, my mama wasn't for the back talk when she was "dealing with me," but she surely stood in my defense against others. I was grateful she knew her daughter, and she knew this wasn't my style. If I got into a fight, there was solid reasoning.

Still, I didn't want my mother going to jail for something I did. I felt guilty and mortified. The humiliation would resurface any time this whole ordeal became the center of a family joke. Family record: "Missy got suspended in Kindergarten for biting a kid." In my mind, I still couldn't fathom how I was a double villain for standing up for myself and mistaking a book bag identical to mine, for my own.

When I returned to school, my teacher expected me to forget any of it had ever happened. I wasn't mad at Carmisha but then Kayla had the audacity to try and partner with me on a group project.

Considering my academic work alone, I was distinguished. We had an awards assembly quarterly. I received multiple trophies and certificates for honor roll and other categories. So the "bad girl" stigma soon faded. Still, I was not okay with working with Kayla. The teacher recommended I be friendlier. I let that advice go in one ear and out the other. I didn't feel like I should be told such thing all because I was perfectly okay with keeping distance.

Of course, the teacher felt compelled to mend things. When we began our science projects of caterpillar metamorphosis, she paired me with Kayla out of the other twenty-one kids she could have chosen. I despised her for it but I knew I couldn't do anything to change it. For the next three weeks, an uncomfortable workspace had developed, and we rarely communicated amongst awkward silences.

On day twenty-one, we went outside to watch our critters grow wings and fly. Everyone laughed as the caterpillar tussled. The peculiar sight of struggle made for a good joke. I anticipated the heavenly wings. The fight for something so beautiful kept me attentive.

"Why the caterpillar have to suffer first?" Camera said with frustration. She went to cover her mouth as she caught herself thinking aloud.

"Same reason I'm stuck in a work group I would rather not be," I leaned toward her and said in a low voice.

"You there because the teacher said so," Camera remarked.

"Yep." I sighed.

THAT'S JUST THE WAY IT IS.

CHAPTER TWO

SUMMER RAIN

For the next two summers, I spent nearly every day at Mama's house. Mama is what we called my grandma. Not just the family but friends of the family; and neighbors alike. Mama's house is the place to be. She lived in a six-flat apartment building. Just like our family, her neighbors along with their big families had lived there for years.

Mama's apartment nor the entire building was ever dull. It was very rare you would show up and not see a house full of her grandkids, great-grandkids, and even great-greats. Many of my older cousins knew that no matter how late they "ran the streets" - as Mama would say - they could go Mama's place and be sure to get in. It was not the same with my aunts and mom. When their doors locked for the night, that was it. Mama's apartment was the family's safe haven. Since Mama's house was walking distance from Wadsworth, we got to visit quite often during the school year too.

Summertime was bussin' more. Probably because everybody was more likely to follow similar agendas. Since school was out for break, we had routines. Most days, we would wake up, have a roast session (make jokes about each other for entertainment), go to the candy store across the alley, and then hang outside. We got frequent visits from our more distant relatives then too. We ran in packs and made up fun as we went. Most days we all walked to Ellis Park to hang out. My older cousins hooped at the court. The younger members played in the park that was barely set apart from the court by a gray chain-linked fence. We practically owned that park. My family had marked those neighborhood streets before my time. And I can't count how many times I've bruised my legs climbing the apparatus or how many times I fell off the monkey bars. Once climbing became an easy task, us kids got creative and began to walk and run over them in games of tag.

My grandma had stayed on 64th and Ellis for years before moving a few blocks east to 65th and Woodlawn Ave. My mom and her kids lived in an apartment on 61st and University for a few years and my Auntie Ruth and Auntie Ann stayed around the corner from us on 62nd St., in separated apartments. Auntie Ruth was the third oldest of my grandma's children, she used to take my cousins, siblings, and I to the lakefront to feed the birds when we were younger. As I got older, we developed more of a work-relationship. Auntie Ann is my grandma's third youngest. She's the "mean" auntie. She was big on manners and yelled excessively when she felt someone weren't showing them. Her biggest pet peeve was entering someone's home without speaking.

Most of my family, were within a one-mile radius of each other. Although my grandma, mom, and aunts shuffled apartments throughout the years, we stayed in the same neighborhood for most of my life. My grandma did anyway, and her place was always "the family house". The neighborhood later known as Dro City—that was our home.

When Ellis Park bored us, we would hang out down towards 62nd and University or at the Midway Plaisance where the middle-high class—mostly White people—enjoyed bike riding and ice skating. Eventually, other kids like us from the neighborhood, linked up with their bikes too. We used to get a kick out of being chased by the security cops, although, we rarely ever knew why they were chasing us out of the area.

Other days we chilled out on Wadsworth grass field playing tackle football or "Run-Chief-Run". Run-Chief-Run is every man for himself. It's similar to freeze tag except you have to make it from one end of the field to the other. We didn't have any youth development centers or Boys and Girls Clubs in the area. When those games got boring, we brainstormed ideas like racing tractors or testing out spark plugs. I'm not sure where my cousins found those things but we used to mess around on abandoned buildings, seeing how they worked. One time, we played truth or dare with the spark plugs. It was our way of forcing somebody to be the person to test the waters. My older cousin had heard the spark plugs can break glass and we were all curious. I dared my cousin to throw it at a huge window of an abandoned building. The dare was almost a no brainer because all he was handed was a small piece of ceramic from the spark plug. My cousin threw the tiny piece at the window and the glass shattered instantly. We were in shock. Every one of us sprinted back towards my grandma's place, hoping no one noticed us. Just as the sun went down, we'd opt in for hide and seek. We knew those jacked streetlights were likely to come on. At least for a short while. Our streetlights rarely worked, and we caught blackouts more often than not. We loved it though. We would run to Mr. Brown's, our closest neighborhood convenient store. At Mr. Brown's we racked up on snacks for the night.

Whenever the streetlights came on we wanted to keep clear of the older folks who hung out on the apartments' porch before they took notice that it was getting late. As soon as we argued amongst each other about somebody not playing fair it was a wrap. Everybody would get sent inside.

By the end of the night, I'd creep in my grandma's room and crawl in bed with her.

"Chile, y'all still out rippin' and runnin'?" my grandma asked as she cleaned her glasses using the fabric of her nightgown.

She always knew it was me. I was the only person who got in bed with her and sometimes, my younger cousin Tulu did too.

"They in the front room," I'd say.

By "they" I meant whoever got sent in while the older teenagers and adults still hung out front talking and drinking or what not.

Mama never slept with her television on. Instead, she had a radio that played the news or some of her favorite shows. Yes, entire sitcom-like shows via radio. I caught myself laughing in my sleep a number of times from the humor of them.

Come morning, Mama was up and out of bed before me. By the time I got up, she would have her television on, sitting in her chair watching the news or Cops. I'd peek up.

Mama saw me out her peripheral and would say to me, "Chile, you up?" she paused briefly, still into her tv show.

"You slept real good," she teased and continued with a smile on her face, "Just'a torsin' and torn'in, torn'in and tors'in." She picked up her newspaper and turned to the page with the tv guide.

I laughed as I stretched and wiped the drool from my cheek, "What's on the tv?"

"I'm watching these crackbrained fools get chased down on Cops."

Sometimes, her southern accent was more prevalent than other times. I'd chuckle and drop my face back into the bed with little remembrance of my tossing around, except the days I woke up at the foot of the bed. Her bed always made me feel like I was sleeping on the clouds. She kept it dressed in several blankets and comforters. Couple that with being beside your protector, knowing that if a boogieman thought to come after you, he wouldn't make it through the gates. I was in heaven!

Cops had tickled Mama enough. She flicked between the news and her soap operas as she sipped her Maxwell's coffee. Once Mama was done with her coffee, she was up and moving. Cleaning and cooking. So this was my cue to have my final stretch and get out of bed, prepared to go on my morning store-run. Usually for tissue and other toiletries that she needed since she didn't buy things by the bulk anymore. With a house full of family, quite often things grew legs and walked out, as Mama would put it. Mama was the kindest, yet she was very clever when it came to taking care of herself. She bought as she needed, and she never went without. Mama handed me a ten-dollar bill and I headed out to Mr. Brown's.

On my way back from the store, Mama had made her way downstairs, sweeping and collecting pennies. That was her way of keeping an eye on me. Even though I wasn't worried since we knew the whole neighborhood, she knew how quick things can happen. Just as Mama was heading back upstairs to her living room window seat, Aunt Tootie and her boys (our more distant relatives) rolled up. My three boy cousins, Todey, Shabazz, and Pez were Aunt Tootie's grandkids. The brothers were actually my second cousins. Their mom is my aunt's daughter. She had six kids, all boys. The older three had lived with Aunt Tootie my whole life. They all lived in Indiana for a few years. The boys, excited to be in the city, raced to the corner store to get Hot Flamin's with nacho cheese, Now and Laters, and whatever other junk food they craved. City convenient stores were exclusive. Many things they sold couldn't be found on the outskirts.

Meanwhile, Aunt Tootie wobbled her way upstairs following Mama. Like most of my older aunt's, she had bad hips and knees. There was a heavy step to match.

It had to have been the second she opened the door that Tulu jumped up and came running downstairs. Knowing him, I'm sure he hadn't brushed his teeth. Tulu is my younger cousin that had the superpower of hearing familiar voices in his sleep that prompted him it was action time. As he landed the bottom step, Aunt Tootie's boys approached the porch with their snacks. Right on time for Tulu. He requested some of everything they opened - per usual. He could eat your mama out of a house and a home.

Blatantly ignoring him, the boys munched down as if they weren't sure they'd see another meal.

"Let's play "It", Todey suggested.

Todey was the oldest of the boys.

The others yelled, "Not it!" in near unison.

"You playing?" he asked me.

"Nah, I got on a skirt." I looked down at my clothes.

I actually had on a skort. A skort is a skirt with shorts attached underneath. Made perfectly for a tomboy like myself. I wasn't in the mood to play around in the outfit, though. I preferred chill out in my hand-me-down skort set that had gotten too little for my big sister, Artika. When we played "It" there were typically no boundaries for hiding spots. I wasn't your ordinary behind a tree kind of girl, either. I'd jump gates, climb on rooftops, and hide in trash cans. It wasn't that kind of a day for me. I took pride in wearing my sister's old set. She used to rock it so well on her tall, slim frame. She danced and cheered, so she naturally had a model-like posture. Me? Not quite. I was the flipper, jumper, runner.

"Let's play hide-n-seek then?" Todey suggested. "We'll stay on the block."

The difference between "Hide-n-Seek" and "It" is that you have time to seek out a hiding spot. In "It" there's rarely an opportunity to hide. Instead, we would run all over the place hoping not to get tagged. You were lucky if the person who's "It" goes to chase someone else before they came after you.

"Fine. Not It!" I agreed.

"NOT ITTT!" My cousins raced to the punch.

"Alright put y'all hand in the fishbowl," I called for everybody to gather around me. As I reached the bottom of the porch, I extended my arms out to make an "O" shape that served as a fish bowl. I wasn't sure if any of them knew about this gimmick. Sometimes there were too many of us to use "Eenie, Meenie, Miney, Mo" or "Bubble Gum, Bubble Gum". My older cousins used to use this method to decide who's "It" first.

"Everyone put a hand in the fish bowl" I directed them all. The boys followed directions.

"Ok, now, somebody put one in for me," I tried to keep from giggling.

For a minute, nobody budged. I asked again.

"Come on, somebody put a hand in for her." Todey co-signed as if he was on to this method.

"I do it," Tulu laughed in uncertainty as he put his other hand in the "bowl".

(Tulu's speech was effected by what is known as tongue-tie. With tongue-tie, he had a shorter than normal lingual frenulum, which made it difficult for him to lift his tongue.)

"You it!" everybody chanted as we guffawed and ran off.

Since Tulu put both of his hands in, he was to be "It". That's the catch of the "fish bowl".

Tulu laughed with us. He knew there had to be something to it. He went to a nearby tree to count. In my mind, I already had my hiding spot established before we took off. I jetted through the gangway. I jumped down the three-four steps and posted up in the corner of the under passage. I stood there chuckling as I could hear the boys struggling to find a good hiding spot.

Just as Tulu hit ten, Todey came running down the steps.

"I'ma stay here," he whispered.

I shook my head no. He didn't budge. It was a tight spot. I didn't want him to get me caught. I wanted so bad to push him out in the opening, but Tulu's voice sounded like it was getting closer. I stood still as my heart went into double-time.

"Ayy!" I felt something crawling on my upper thigh. Instinctively, my leg jerked.

"Shhh," Todey expressed as if I was gone blow the hiding spot.

I stood upright again. Not even thirty seconds later and there was another tickle. This time I noticed, as clear as day, my cousin's fingers sweeping my leg. As warm as it was out, chills passed through my body in a flash, giving me goosebumps.

Tulu hopped down into the underpass, and called out, "Aye, wea e'body at?"

Todey was startled. "That was too fast." He jumped in front of Tulu and demanded that he go recount.

"Un-uhnn," Tulu objected.

"Yea, you don't have to count again," I confirmed with Tulu.

"Okay, okay, I recount," Tulu bargained.

"No, I quit." I concluded.

The other two boys had found hiding spots elsewhere but came out when they heard chatter. They followed me around front pleading for me to play another round as if four people wasn't enough. I hardly caught anything they said. I was still in arm's reach but mentally long gone.

I went upstairs, bypassing the family and activities taking place in the front room. I went and laid in Mama's bed, pretending to watch television. After some time of a show watching me, I dozed off.

When I woke up Aunt Tootie, and her boys had gone and got lost in the woods. I hoped so anyway. I had never been to their place. I just knew they stayed out in Indiana in a trailer park that Mama always referred to as the boon-docks. A place I imagined as a cave - dark, cold, and lonely. We had no trailer parks in the city, and I had never seen anything like it. I hoped they were there already though. And that coyotes and bears troubled them. Besides, Aunt T wasn't easy going herself. Granted, she is the eldest of my grandma's bunch. She's very bossy and demanding. She comes around once every blue moon and often thinks there's only one way to spell right.

For hours on end, I picked my brain trying to figure out the logic of her grandson. Doesn't he know we're family? Was that part of the plan when he initiated the idea of playing tag? Why didn't I say anything to him? I should've told Mama. Would Aunt T have defended his wrongs? I remember how she always stood up for her boys if someone else attempted to correct them.

By nightfall, I allowed these thoughts to escape. I stored the events in the back of my mind and never spoke on them to anyone. Not even Mama.

CHAPTER THREE

READY OR NOT

By THIRD GRADE, WE MOVED TO A NICE TOWNHOME OUT in Hammond, Indiana. Two bathrooms, a double-entry kitchen, and a balcony that allowed you to overlook the multiple shades of green grass. The most beautiful thing we had ever even partially possessed was the ever-relaxing water flow from the river stream out back.

We moved in mid-summer and got comfortable in a flash. For the first time, my siblings and I had to split up and attend different schools. My twin brother, Allante, and I were enrolled at the elementary school. My older brother and sister attended the middle school. In the city, all of the neighborhood schools were Kindergarten through eighth grade, so everyone was together. It wasn't like we hung together when we were all going to the same school. We all had our own friends. Still, in all, this was different. These schools were predominantly white.

I draped my head from the foot of my bed one night and stared at the ceiling. My big sister's bed sited, parallel to mine, directly across our 220 square feet bedroom. She lounged on her big, plush pillow and watched America's Next Top Model.

"What's wrong?" My sister asked as she took notice of my mood when her show came to a commercial break.

"Mm, not much, just thinking," I voiced.

"You sure? You've been staring at the ceiling for thirty minutes straight," my sister persisted.

"Well... it's just that... I dream of a place where people doesn't have to pretend about who they are and what they like or dislike," I said to her.

"Did something happen at school today?" Tika questioned.

"Yea, you see, at first it didn't bother me that there weren't many other Black kids in that school. But I noticed one minute the students there are friendly and other times they flat out ignore me. It's kinda mindboggling," I expressed.

"Really? That would annoy me, too," Tika reckoned.

"I was cool with it. Seemed like I was being treated like any other student, you know?" I continued.

"Sure. Some kids talked to you and stuff, right?" Tika asked.

"Only when others are not around, it seems."

"That's not right. And you don't have to talk to them, we have each other," my sister reassured me.

"Yea, it's not that. It just annoys me that when I try to stay to myself, they go out their way to speak and talk to me individually. I don't get that. It's almost like they can't be seen talking to me." I explained.

"Well you're not obligated to respond. Maybe, next time, give them a piece of your mind."

"Yea, you're right," I concluded.

My sister continued to watch ANTM as the judges

announced the models who would proceed to the next round. I repositioned myself in bed and plugged my head-phones in my ears.

I felt a sense of relief when I witnessed it wasn't just me that were receiving awkward vibes from some of the residents in our new town.

Later that evening, I went with my mama to the grocery store. Upon checkout, we encountered a woman with an unpleasant attitude. The White woman slapped my mama's change down on the counter instead of handing it to her.

"Excuse me; can you place my money in my hand?" My mama suggested.

The woman looked down at the counter and attempted to blow my mama off, "Just take it."

"Just as I placed the cash in your hand-to purchase- is just how I expect you to return the change to me." My mama requested.

The White woman released an exaggerated exhale and told my mama "You're holding up my line." Then she went to reach for the next customer's items.

"No ma'am, that's not how we gone do this. You will not ring up another item until I speak with your supervisor. Now, what you can do is go get him or her," my mama commanded.

The woman rolled her eyes before my mama finished her sentence and walked to the back of the store. She returned with her store manager.

"Hi, ma'am. Sorry about the inconvenience, here's your change." The store manager attempted to rush us off with a seemingly reluctant apology.

"Sir, I'm gonna need your store number and the number to corporate." My mama requested. She had been a supervisor at several department stores and she was not content with how the situation was handled.

The next day at school, I found myself feeling alone in a crowd again. The fact that my twin and I had different lunch periods didn't help at all. Our cafeteria was twice the size as my old school, and lunch was open seating versus the assigned table seating I was accustomed to. I hated the way some of the people- students and staff- focused on me as if I was some foreigner. So, I would slither through and sit as close to the food tray line as possible.

Casey and a friend of hers sat down in two of the five empty seats at the table with me. Casey was a blonde hair girl who sometimes spoke and talked to me in our Reading class.

"Hey Casey". I said dryly, as I noticed the irritated look on her friend's face.

"Hey," Casey uninhibited a quick smirk and slowly placed her tray on the table. Her gaze searched the cafeteria. The room filled with third, fourth, and fifth graders, as pop music played in the background. Two other kids, girl and boy, walked up with their food trays in hands. The girl had two pigtails with a bang that was growing pass her eyebrows. The boy was slim and tall for his age. He wore a baseball cap with the brim backwards and glasses. They stood behind their chair and placed their trays on the table, as their eyes communicated with Casey's shrugged shoulders and raised eyebrows.

"Hey, you can't sit here, this is our table," the boy said.

"But I thought it was open seating" I responded in confusion as I ate a scoop of applesauce.

"Yea, but we sit here every day, sooo.." The little skinny boy raised one eyebrow.

"It's fine, she can stay," Casey intervened in a careful tone.

"Oh, I see. Yea, now I know for tomorrow. Just sit right there." I pointed at the empty seats at the table.

"No, this is our table. Right, Ms. Valdez?" He nudged one of the lunchroom helpers as she walked by.

Ms. Valdez was a member of the Parent Teacher Association. She often volunteered in the cafeteria and on the school buses.

"That's right, you can eat over there." Ms. Valdez directed me to move.

"Well I'm already half way done eating. We can all sit here or there's other open tables, too."

The lunch lady walked off with a look of disgrace. She posted up on the wall side by side with another lady and spoke with a paper covering her mouth as she frequently glanced over in our direction. My refusal to move when told to, by the kid and woman, led to often strange looks from staff and parents. Then, everyone knew who the new kid was.

I don't have much recollection at this school. Frankly, can't even tell you the name of the place. I do remember that at that school, I felt discredited and dishonored. I felt like I wasn't nearly as intellectual as my unbroken honor roll status at Wadsworth Elementary had deemed me to be.

I was required to do a prolonged one-on-one reading comprehension exam with my teacher. The teacher pulled me out of class, to the hallway, while our class was in the middle of movie-time. She had a single chair set up along the wall and a tote of books on the floor.

"We're going to be reading a few books throughout the day. Everyone gets a chance to come out here, so don't worry. It's not graded we're just here to measure where you are," Ms. Macklin explained to me.

"Okay," I said readily as I saw her reach for the Junie B. Jones book. Those were my favorite book series to read.

She then sat her timer and prompted me to read a passage before starting it. Knowing this was a timed test, I sped through.

"Great timing!" she congratulated me.

We did this twice more throughout the day. We read passages from The Mouse and The Motorcycle and Charlotte's Web.

As I finished Charlotte's Web my teacher cheered me on again, "Fantastic!"

"Now, let's see how well you understand what you read?" Ms. Macklin carried on and instructed me to make several inferences about the stories. I remembered things like the titles, authors, main ideas, protagonist and antagonist, and could even summarize each of the books. She wanted more though. Ms. Macklin wanted me to read between the lines. To take words for anything more than face value, especially in a given amount of time, was a new concept for me. I could read quickly enough to be done in the time allotted. Or I could take however much time I needed to comprehend and analyze the story. I wasn't given much time.

After a while, I grew flustered, "Ms. Macklin, what's the point in making a story out to be something that it's not?"

I simply could not grasp the point in this concept. I just wanted to enjoy the Junie B. Jones book. Besides, at home, anything my mama meant she said just that. In fact, all of my family did.

Not considering it a cry for help, the teacher made it

clear she ran things in her classroom and didn't owe a kid an explanation.

She shot back, "It's simple Ashante. With the directions I gave, you just have to complete the assignment the best you can."

"I'm not sure I understand. Why do we have to do this?" I questioned.

"You know it's simple, I gave you instructions and if it's not figured out when I come back we'll make this a phone call home." The teacher grew flustered.

I didn't quite register her message well. My youth emotions were all over by now, and I loss of the slightest bit of attentiveness left inside of me. Delivering her promise, the teacher called home and reported my "lack of effort". According to my teacher, (even though she told me I read fluently) my reading level was equivalent to my peers that were two grades below.

My mama knew how much I missed my old school and concluded my infractions reflected that. She had simply warned me that if I didn't cut the nonsense, I'd be in hot water. My mama knew nothing about the previous incident I had during lunch. The school didn't report it, and I didn't bother telling her either.

The next day at school, I daydreamed most of the day away. In Reading class, Casey took notice of my aloofness when Ms. Macklin directed the class to get into groups.

"Hey, want to work with me?" Casey asked.

"Sure," I responded, laconically. I noticed both kids that Casey normally talks with were absent. I figured that's the only reason she asked me to partner with her.

"Are you gonna come over?" She asked.

"You can sit here." I extended my hand, referencing the

vacant space beside me on the vinyl soft seat. "I don't need any more seating problems, you know?"

"Sorry, that kid is always being bossy" Casey gathered her supplies and came over to my table.

"Why you sorry, you can only control yourself." I eased up.

"You're right but he only does that because his mom works here and is a part of the PTA." Casey acknowledge.

"Who's his mom? And what is PTA?" I probed.

"Ms. Valdez. The Parent Teacher Association is an organization where the parents are a part of everything that goes on in the school and make big decisions." Casey answered

"Go figure."

"Are most of these kids that way? And is that why you talk to me only sometimes? Because of your friends?" I inquired.

"Well, I'm a friendly person and you are nice too. I told Kaley how pretty you were on the first day you got here and that you should be our friend. So no, it's not that, it's just--" Casey empathized in a sincere tone before the teacher interrupted her.

"How's it going over here, Casey?" The teacher asked as she glanced at me, certainly not making direct eye contact.

"Good," Casey pretended she had been working. Ms. Macklin continued to roam the classroom.

"Hopefully everyone got to a good stopping point, let's wrap up and we'll pick up tomorrow." Ms. Macklin announce.

When the bell rang for us to go to our next class, I was frustrated. I felt like the teacher didn't acknowledge to my mama that I legit tried my best nor did she extend me any help. I felt like she knew she was wrong for that, too.

Moving forward, I began to ask so many questions during classwork time that the teacher found it to be deliberate and annoying. When I finally told my twin what I had been dealing with in Reading class that what he suggested, so I tried it. After several more mishaps—granted, I over analyzed some "problems" after the initial incident—I found asking questions actually was an adequate learning style for me. I questioned everything that I needed to for better understanding. Although everything I inquired was valid, and many other students looked for some of the same information, it was mistaken for a challenge. Most of the other kids just went with the flow of any given lesson. When I questioned, they would then make their confusions known. The teacher started ignoring me and some days she opted to have us "hold questions until the end". Most times, we had forgotten our questions by then. I started writing mine down. Soon after, I noticed the teacher would leave out the room as soon as the bell rung.

One day, Ms. Macklin announced, "to help everyone, we will begin to take notes from the lessons and use our notes on the quizzes. After the quizzes are graded I will return them for y'all to use as a study guide for the exam." Our exams consisted of multiple quizzes compiled- exact same questions. That didn't help my understanding of the material. Carter G. Woodson once said, "To handicap a student by teaching him that his Black face is a curse and that his struggle to change his condition is hopeless is the worst sort of lynching." In that same respect, stripping a child of their inquiring mind and curiosity is just as bold an attempt.

I observed patterns early on. When questioned, teachers were often either tongue-tied or speechless, unable to effectively deliver their lessons. Maybe they didn't quite know themselves what it was they were teaching. Their job merely required following a layout and keeping students "under control". It can be difficult to remember which is more important when superiority is a priority. Furthermore, grading is almost strictly reliant on an answer book. Yeah, that "Teacher's Edition". So academically speaking, the teacher has a degree and answers. Therefore, she's safe.

As for the student, I started to wonder if the concept of rote learning a given topic outweighed how to think and develop new ideas. My progress report reflected an improvement in my grades and behavior since I simply memorized notes versus questioning the information. I didn't have much to say in class anymore. I began to seek interest elsewhere.

When test day came, I didn't need to understand the material to look like a scholar. Rather, my remembrance of "lessons" reviewed determined if I was READY OR NOT.

CHAPTER FOUR

THE BURBS

My alarm clock must've been awake all night waiting to sing for me.

Some boys at the school out in Indiana stole Tony's book bag and gym shoes. And that was my mama's last straw. She was fed up at the fact that even surveillance couldn't get his possessions back to him. Not only that but we were facing prejudices throughout the community. The schools had also been giving my mama a tough time about us riding the school buses. I never learned why. We had just found out my mama was expecting my baby brother. So, we moved back to the city and used my grandad's address to enroll in the suburban school district.

At 5:45am I woke up to a dress nicely ironed, laid out across the foot of my pink, twin sized, bunk-bed. There were tights and a blouse along with it. All ready to hug me. The clothes were pretty but the thought of wearing them saddened me. This was my mama's way of helping me get in touch with my girly side. I couldn't stay out the mirror because of how beautiful I looked. When I got to school the boys made comments all day long. Some teased me because they figured it wasn't by choice that I was wearing this stuff. The way I slouched down to shy away from attention was confirming enough. Others gave one too many compliments and stared at me relentlessly. I loathed the recognition. It made me feel out of place. I was very bashful. I told my mama I didn't want to wear skirts and dresses anymore. I never told her why. So, there were more dress-wearing days of course. I got to a point where I started to pack my pants and gym shoes inside my book bag. I took the extra clothes with me. I used to change in the school bathroom, before the tardy bell rung. I came home with ripped tights too often. My mama eventually let me pick out my own clothes. She said I was being too rough. I always had to rush to change, out in the morning and back into my skirts before I made it home. My toenails would snag runs into my tights that led to holes. It didn't help at all when I had to change clothes in the tiny space of a bathroom stall. My mama was right. I was being too rough rushing and changing in those tiny spaces.

Catch-a-girl-kiss-a-girl was the peak of the day for the typical fourth grader at Dikeman Elementary. Catch–a-girl-kiss-a-girl, was a game played every day during recess. There was that and there was football. Nearly every day I was the only girl on the field.

One day, at my-still relatively new- school, I didn't want to be bothered with wrestling over the football. I played on the park slides by myself and exchanged dialogue with some of the girls as they posted up near me pretending to flee the boys. They whispered and laughed.

"We see you peeking through the tic-tac-toe," one of the girls yelled at a boy. I laughed at the outburst as I turned to peep the joke. It was a relief to be semi-local again, with peers more relatable.

Out of nowhere, Clifford ran up behind me grasping my waist. Insulted and embarrassed, I socked him in the face. That was enough for him to loosen his grip. I snatched away and turned to fight him.

For the first time in years, I relived the touching of my cousin's warm fingers crawling on my thigh. Only thing I knew was that it wouldn't happen again.

"Hey, hey! Wh--what's th-the m-matter w-with you two?" Mr. Kroger shouted as he grabbed Clifford by the arm. Mr. Kroger was my fourth grade teacher. He was an old white man with a hunched back and white hair, and had a bad stuttering problem. He often lashed out over small things or at the wrong kids because students ran over him on the regular.

"Man, let me go! She hit me." Clifford yelled at the teacher as he snatched away.

"W-what's g-going on here!!?" Mr. Kroger shouted at me. "N-nevermind, b-both of –y-you t-to the office." He sent us both inside to speak with the principal. Expectantly, Clifford and I both had to serve two-hour after school detention. Clifford for playing too rough, once he told the principal it was all over a game of tag. And me, for what my principal described to me as an "assault". That was my first time hearing the term assault, and I was terrified when the principal said it could ultimately lead to someone going to jail. By this time, I was good at not telling my mama about my troubles at school. If the school didn't report it, it was left unsaid. With the pregnancy of my baby brother, my mama had enough to deal with on her own, I figured. I didn't want to add on to any stress, in any way.

I felt like I had to stay away from boys or befriend them

in such ways that would keep them from crushing on me. I began to hang out with the fellas. Clifford was teased about "getting beat up by a girl" for a few days, then we became friends. I started to hang out with him and his boys, and he treated me like his little sister.

The burbs had become a fun hangout spot for my siblings and I, before going home to our city apartment. School used to let out at 2:30. My mama worked till five or six in the evening. So, we had a few hours to hang around. Or serve detention. All my siblings joined some type of afterschool activities. My brother played sports, my sister was on the debate team and the cheerleading team, and I was too shy for sports or any activities that required a crowd of attention. Except that one time I was asked to cover for someone in the school district's Spelling Bee. I wasn't at the school when the original contestants were selected. I just remembered hearing some of the kids talk about the contest. I was nervous when I learned that the Spelling Bee would be held that same evening. But I was eager to participate because I knew my mama would come out to support and cheer me on. I was given two hours to look over the packet of spelling words that the other students had been studying for the last four weeks. It was nerve wrecking. I won the contest and was filled with joy. My mama was proud. She took me to get food and ice cream and bought me a brand new bicycle.

Most days, though, I hung around the school drawing or listening to music. I got acquainted with a few more people from school. The suburban areas were different. It wasn't half as high-risk as the city. In the suburbs, we met up with each other and hung at the different parks. Or at our friends' houses, playing the game and jumping on trampolines.

. . .

WE MADE it through my seventh-grade year in the suburban school district. Things were actually smooth sailing. I made long-term friends who were relatable. Academically, I was placed in all advanced placement classes. Coursework wasn't as easy as my first school, but things were challenging enough, and there was teachers' support in academic achievement. I felt as if I was much more adept at dealing with the material here than I was out in Indiana, at my predominantly white elementary school. My competency reflected again through my honor roll status. I was happy to feel smart again.

Once my mama came home from the hospital with my baby brother it wasn't long before we transferred back to the city closer to her workplaces and family. My siblings and I rode the CTA and PACE buses just to attend a decent school. Waking up at 4am got to be overwhelming, and some days, we didn't get home until six in the evening. My mama researched new neighborhoods and school districts for quite some time.

CHAPTER FIVE

IN THE CITY

In the Englewood area, popularity grew rapidly for my siblings and me. Many people was keen to Allante because he was a laid-back kid and into sports, Artika was pretty and stayed fresh to death. Although, I was reserved, people gravitated towards me because I was fun to hang around with a "take-no-shit" demeanor.

As the weather began to break, the Salvation Army Center became our kick-it spot. During the week, there was open gym from six until nine at night. We made it habit to come home from school and do our chores and homework just in time to hang out there.

Most days all of the girls sat courtside chatting and cheerleading as the fellas bust sweats up and down the court. At home, Artika and I talked messed to Allante about his ballgame but at the center, we couldn't wait to hooray for the most effortless lay-up or rebound. There was so much excitement for me in watching the guys attempt to break ankles and dunk on one another. The stadium occasionally shook whenever somebody got dunked on or got their shot beat to the middle of next week.

Chrishaun, better known in the neighborhood as City was one of the best dribblers on the court. His shot was A1, too. I had been eyeing him for a week or so. I was intrigued by how he took his talent seriously on the court yet didn't let any mishaps send him into an outrage. Well, that's if we disregard that one day his team lost because their big man let a lil guy get the rebound and score a bucket. Chrishaun stormed off the court in my direction, adrenaline rushing.

"These dudes so weak Missy!" he said in a voice that made it difficult to decipher if he was really pissed or not.

I didn't pay that too much attention though. I was caught by the fact that he knew my name. My heartbeat skipped a beat. I settled quickly, once he prolonged the nag about the game as he took his hooping shoes off.

He went back and forth with a few of the other fellas that weren't quite in the vicinity of his voice range. They were all riled up, unattractively. As I got up to leave the gym with my sister, City paused in the middle of his rebuttal to one of the players and asked me to tie his shoe in a joking manner.

"You got me messed up," I looked back and said, as I rolled my eyes. I walked off laughing on the inside. I thought he was so corny, but it was cute. I pondered all night, about how I didn't know how to flirt back. The one time a dude I actually liked tries to flirt, I blew it.

A few days later, after pretending I didn't exist, seemingly getting closer to my brother and sister though, City attempted to talk to me again. For the first time, I saw Khalia in the center. Khalia and I were in the same class at my new school, Wentworth Elementary. Her assigned seat was right across from mine. Seated correctly at our desks, we'd have no choice but to look each other right in the face. We were bound to one another. Khalia was impulsive and exceptionally outspoken. Fortunately, we vibed instantly off our niche for respect. I went and sat by her in the bleachers.

"Yoooo, what's up cuzo?" City said excitedly when he saw Khalia.

"What's good cuzo?" Khalia responded with a smile.

They engaged in small talk for all of two minutes. Chrishaun blocked my view of the court.

"Excuse me." I said

"Oh-oh, my bad Miss Lady." He said with a smirk.

"Cuzo, you know her?" He continued.

"Yea this my girl, G. She just moved over here."

He whispered in Khalia's ear and she laughed. I shook my head.

"But naw cuzo, fa'real." He concluded.

"Don't be talking behind my back," I joked.

"I was just—um—telling her how you treated me the other day."

"Ummhm." I muttered.

City carried on, as he inquired my age and grade, all of the things I figured he already knew by then. In return, I asked every question he asked, in total nervousness. Television may have been great help then because I was not equipped on what to say or how to "go with the flow." I learned that City was a grade above and two years older than I. I said things that made him uncomfortable, I'm certain, but I was crushing on him. When he parted I asked Khalia what was up with him.

"That's cuzo. He cool. He wants you, girl. But sis can tell you better than me, I be in my own zone." Khalia said as she pointed to a beautiful brown, afro-wearing girl that approached us on the bleachers.

"This my sister Patrice. Trice, this my girl Missy who I told you remind me of you. City tryna talk to her." Khalia exclaimed as I sat quietly feeling embarrassed.

I didn't know Khalia's sister like that and wasn't comfortable with Khalia introducing us in that way. I didn't want Patrice thinking I was stuck-up just because a boy around there was attracted to me. Patrice was cool about it though, "girrrrl, don't do it." She laughed, "I'm just playing. You is pretty. You and cuzo would look good together."

I released a light laugh, "Yea he cute but I'm cool." What I really wanted to ask was, why did she said don't do it, but I was still a little timid. Patrice is Khalia's big sister. Totally opposite of Khalia, Patrice is soft-spoken and patient with a heart of gold. She is two years older than I am, and a school grade higher—same as Chrishaun. Soon enough, Khalia, Patrice, and myself all started meeting at the park or the center after school. I was not ready to start discussing boys with my sister so I opened up to Patrice. It was also helpful that she and City were cousins. Patrice was all for minding her business but would not dare let me fall sucker to any shenanigans.

Three days later, Chrishaun and I exchanged numbers and talked on the phone for hours throughout the night. By the end of summer, beginning my Freshman year of high school, I had myself a boyfriend.

Once the school year started, we were in each other's presence daily. He was still very much a people's person and from the looks, a lady's man too. We'd post up together at games, or after school, and girls would come by dragging his name as they spoke. Everybody loved this dude. I didn't like it. Chrishaun's personality was delightful, so it was no wonder people loved being in his company. But it had me backing off.

Everyday, Chrishaun and I met up by my locker before and after our lunch periods. Most times, he'd catch me off guard while I was in my locker. Today I heard his voice as I turned the corner. He must've beat me because my teacher lectured a few minutes past the bell. When I got to my locker aisle, Chrishaun was acting silly, laughing and running in the opposite direction of me. I was running late for my next class, so I didn't bother calling for him.

Rushing to my seat, I caught a glimpse of Shaquilla's notebook. I must've been tweaking though. It couldn't have possibly read what I thought it did. Plus, I just walked past her in the hall. How did her supplies get on her desk already? I am tripping.

Shaquilla came inside less than two minutes later, blushing and snickering. And certainly, sat right at her assigned desk. She must have dropped her things off before the bell rang. We often did that when we knew we were gonna be late, to keep the teacher from taking notice of our tardiness. Our teacher had left just before class started to make copies of an assignment. So she was good on that note. That's probably why she was so happy, right? Saved by the bell.

When the teacher came back in, he read off his roster for attendance. Everyone simply said, "Here," or something along the lines of it. Once he got to Shaquilla, she raised her arm, notebook in hand, for clear visibility. It read "Mrs. City." My eyes weren't playing tricks on me after all. My stomach sunk as the classroom got so quiet you could hear a pin drop. I felt like all eyes were on me although only a handful were. People looked at me anticipating a reaction. I didn't say anything. There wasn't anything for me to say. Nobody asked me about it directly. Besides, my hardcore ways were still front and center, so I'm sure most people thought I just didn't care.

The guys I regularly socialized with started talking amongst each other about the rumors they had heard about City and Shaquilla. I listened as other people chimed in and one person even threw a few subs at Shaquilla. Others took it as typical high school gossip. Shaquilla did not care. After all, she was a very pretty, brown-skinned, tall girl and was confident in all of her qualities. As long as everybody knew, she was a relevant factor that was all that mattered at that point. Everything else, she laughed around it.

As for me, well I took a hit to the chin. I consciously stayed distant of Shaquilla. We were never the best of friends, but we were cordial. We had many of the same courses and socialized with mutual people. After that, I would only speak to her if she spoke to me and even then, my "heys" were shallow. Tashara probably gets some credit for keeping things balanced because Shaquilla was nonchalant about the whole ordeal. Normally, if I distant myself from a person or do not like a person, I stay away from them and anything that has close ties with them, especially family. Tashara and Shaquilla were sisters, both in the same grade as I. They acted a lot alike. Tashara was more sociable. Her warmhearted jollity spirit made it difficult to be mad at her for long, even if she was the person to direct frustration at for some reason. She always found a way to talk and joke with everybody, and I wasn't excluded. It was as if the whole situation just was not a big deal to them. Eventually, I let it go too and Shaquilla and I were better off.

I didn't bother asking City about the stuff I had heard or seen. I cut all ties. Whenever he tried to talk to me, I was standoffish and pushed him into a friend zone. I was disappointed but it didn't feel like a heartbreak. Once more "rumors" began to surface about Chrishaun; I felt I wasn't even ready to start dating. That was enough for me to resurface as "one of the guys" and keep dudes at a ten-foot distance with no pressure.

I hung out with Terrell, Trevell, and Carter mostly. They were from my neighborhood so we started linking up to catch the 63rd St. bus each morning and afternoon—to and from school. They were all a grade above me, the same grade as Patrice and Chrishaun. Our school was intimate so we all had close ties. Englewood High School Campus actually consisted of two schools in one. TEAM Englewood and Urban Prep Englewood. Starting my sophomore year, school fights often broke out between the two. It was like an all-out war. The fights would break out any time of the day —early mornings, during lunch periods, after school, and sometimes at random when kids started to pull the fire alarm so that both schools could evacuate the building. Although, Urban Prep was an all-boys academy, you can count on Patrice, Kay Kay, and I to stand by our "brothers". That's just the relationship we built with the boys from our hoods. We were like family.

Carter was stocky, and had zero tolerance for bullshit. He joked a lot but everyone knew when he was serious. In school, he was like the hood hero, straight ride or die. Trevell and Terell were twin brothers. I knew them since they were younger. When I transferred to Englewood, Trevell remembered me from when I was a little girl. He and Terrell were amongst the other kids that started hanging out in The Midway Plaisance with my siblings, cousin, and myself. They lived on 62nd and University back then, too. They actually still lived in their same apartment when we got to high school. Terrell was tall with some weight on him and he played football. They had a good head on their shoulders and knew how to adjust from the streets to school. Trevell was mellow and drama free. He knew the value of staying ahead of the game. He played basketball and kept a happy spirit. When the school wars broke out—TEAM Englewood versus Urban Prep—it turned to be about gangs. The neighborhood our school was located in was home of the Black Disciples. Opposed to the neighborhood we grew up in, filled with Gangster Disciples.

———

Prince of Cottage Grove

———

MY MAMA SHOOK ME OUT MY SLEEP. "Wake up, Shay!"

I was tired from a long day at school. I didn't go outside afterwards. Instead, I went straight home and fell asleep still dressed in my school clothes. I moaned and did a lazy roll over. My mama's voice grew distant. She was still saying something. I turned back towards the wall to doze off again.

"Come on Shay! This is not the time. He just got shot in front of my baby," My mama voice was stern, "We have to go get her!"

"Who?" I jumped up from my bed. I walked towards my mama in the front room, where she sat on the couch lacing her shoes.

"Tyquan just got shot in front of Tika," My mama said as she stood up from the couch.

My mama was never good with names. She left me confused and scared. I wiggled my feet into my gym shoes without unlacing them. I stumbled out the door, trying to keep up with my mama as she raced out the building. Our apartment building was near the corner of 66th and Cottage Grove. We turned the corner and saw police lights, red tape and patches of people on Evans—the next block over. My heart began to beat double-time when I saw Tika crying asking why. People had their arm around her trying to guide her away from the scene. I had never seen my sister cry like that.

Tyshawn was my sister's boyfriend. And also, a good friend of my entire family. His family had been in the neighborhood for years, too. He was killed shot in front of Tika, while they were hanging out. She went into instant shock that lasted her a week. I was sick to my stomach because even after the fact, she talked less. She was already reserved but at least we got to communicate. I knew the things she liked and didn't like. I knew how to get her to open up. I saw the change in her and it hurt me that I couldn't do anything to help her. I felt like she was becoming a different person and I didn't know this new version of her. It took her months to go back to her normal self.

Tyshawn's mother and sisters used to check on my sister from time to time. His younger sister, Willisha admired Tika. I became friends with Willisha when Tika introduced us. Willisha was a few years younger than me. I used to see her around the neighborhood but we never said much to each other. When Tyshawn passed away, we developed a tight relationship. She became my little sister. We had a lot more in common than we knew. We learned that we both found joy in doing hair and that we didn't want to become products of our environment, most importantly. We started doing each other's hair and using that time to express ourselves to one another. Willisha graduated elementary school and went to Paul Robeson, the same high school Tika attended. Robeson was in the Englewood Community, same as my high school. And they weren't too far from each other. On some days, Willisha and I began to meet up after school and traveled back to our neighborhood together. We hung out and had one another's back, rather it was sharing food or ready to fight for each other.

CHAPTER SIX

RUNNING ON, RUNNING ON

THE AROMA OF NECK BONES ACCOMPANIED BY RAYS OF sun beaming through the tied curtains of Mama's living room never failed to put me in a meditative state. I could hear myself think, I could breathe. I owe some credit to my Auntie Lottie's plants she housed on the windowsills, in Mama's living room. Auntie Lottie was the oldest of my grandmother's bunch. Some people in the family said that she had her own apartment before but as for as long as I can remember, she lived with Mama. Auntie Lottie had inherited the bad hips and knees that ran in the family, too. Her condition was worse than Aunt Tootie's. She was passionate about music and her plants were her babies. She talked to them, sung to them, and delicately cared for them. Every time I came over, Auntie Lottie schooled me on how to nourish them too. Mama's place, in the early morning, tended to be the only place I could find a peace of mind.

It was routine for me to stop by every day on my way to school. Partially because I knew my grandma would be awake. Many days she sat in the window drinking her coffee and could see after me as I went on to the bus stop. I still relied on her protection, especially during the quiet fall mornings where the sun shines from one direction and the sky is gloomy in others.

It had to been the way I sat at the kitchen table, mixing Jiffy, and cleaning greens. This must've signaled to Mama that I needed her. Seems like every time I skipped school, she would give me money and tell me to be safe. I never missed school for the heck of it. Most times I was suspended and I didn't want my mama to find out. I knew she would kick my butt. I often left out in the morning as if I were heading to school, as usual. My grandma had to have had an idea. I used the five or ten dollars she would give me to get me a two dollar transit card. Each two-dollar transit card is usually three bus or train rides if you transfer within two hours. I usually took the 63 St. bus to the Red Line. I remember riding the train from 63rd to Downtown Howard to 95th and back to 63rd St. I did that as many times as I needed to, from 7am until school got out. On those rides, I always sat at the back of the train cart. I took a window seat and placed my book bag on the seat beside me. I didn't want anyone to bother me if I fell asleep. Most times, I did at some point throughout the day. I plugged my headphones in and gazed out the window. I mesmerized at the emphasis of the city. My surroundings transitioned from liquor stores, vacant lots, and abandoned buildings to beautiful green grass, mature trees, and markets with expensive looking storefront signs.

Once I was so hungry, I decided to ride the train opposite of the direction I normally traveled. I headed straight to 95th St. I transferred and took the Pace bus to Calumet City. Auntie Phyllis lived out there now. She left Memphis a couple years after we moved back to Chicago. She stayed a few other places, but eventually settled in a house out in Calumet City. Auntie Phyllis's house stayed stocked with groceries, and she usually worked during the school hours. My cousin, Lena, was normally home during that time. I couldn't be sure, though, so I was risking no one would answer the door. But hey, I had six or seven hours before school let out, and the ride out there took only two. I was used to it from back when I took the bus to and from Diekman Elementary with my siblings.

When I got there, I knocked on the door. My cousin was home. She opened the door after the first knock, without even asking who was there. Lena is Auntie Phyllis's oldest daughter. She's about six years older than I am. And one of the coolest cousins of the family. She used to let us younger cousins have fun and do whatever we liked. Our other older cousins, had their limitations.

"Shayyy!" Lena said happily. "What you doing out here young lady?"

"Dang, can I check up on you?" I snickered, trying to avoid her question.

"Yea, after school hours, ma'am." She shot me down and continued, "Now why are you not there?"

"Long story," I said.

"Yea, well make a long story short". She persisted.

"Well, our school had a fight with the other school so a lot of us got suspended." I explained.

"Aw man, well you know my mama gone be home soon so you might not want to stick around too long." She warned me.

"Yea, I'm not. But ya' girl starving, what's to eat in here?" I asked as I opened the fridge.

"I made pancakes, eggs, and sausage this morning. There's some pancakes left." Lena offered.

"Yuck, no!" I declined.

I loved pancakes but never ate Lena's because she only used this one particular brand of syrup that tasted so disgusting to me. I ate me some Cap'N Crunch Berry's cereal and hung around a bit before I headed back out. I tracked my bus before leaving. Suburban transit didn't run every ten to fifteen minutes like in the city. Their buses came by hourly. In the middle of January, it was too cold out to wait on the bus stop. As I headed out, Auntie Phyllis came moping down the street.

"Hey my favorite niece," she greeted me

"Hey auntie," I muttered back.

What you doing out this way? Ain't no school today?" she asked me.

"No, I'm out today" I replied.

"Good, your auntie need you to go to the store for me. I need me a Pepsi and Mr. Goodbar," she requested.

I fulfilled her request, happily. I was glad she didn't interrogate me any further about school. When I returned with my auntie's goodies, I checked the time for the next bus. I had twenty minutes to wait, but was ready to go. The bus stop was only seven minutes away. I figured I'd get going before I was bombarded with questions.

The gloomy skies and lactose, combined had me drowsy. On the ride back to the city, I slept the entire way, until it was time for me to transfer. I woke up just in time for my exits. I strolled in the house feeling restless.

"You look tired. How was school?" My mama asked. She sat in her room folding clothes as I walked pass her doorway.

"School was cool." I said.

"No homework?" She checked me.

"No, not today." I confirmed. My mama raised from her

bed and entered the living room as I took off my coat and book bag.

"Phyllis called and told she saw you today. Why didn't you tell me y'all had an early release today?" She questioned.

"We didn't." I responded anxiously.

"How the hell you get all the way out there?"

I stood there with a blank face. I didn't have a response.

"Your ass need to start talking" My mama demanded of me.

My hands began to fidget and my lips started to quiver but I remained silent.

"I'm going up to the school in the morning, and if I find out you been skipping school, I'm whooping your ass." My mama made clear.

My mama did just what she said. She went to the school and learned that I had been suspended for over a week and hadn't told her about it. My mama slapped me upside my head and I could not dare ask to go outside.

Soon after, my mama decided to move us to Minnesota, to be away from familiarity. She wanted us to focus on our priorities. At 15, I got to Minnesota and was able to secure an hourly paying job, in no time. And a second job a few weeks later, when school let out for summer break.

I transferred from TEAM to Austin High school in a small country town out in Minnesota.

I sat in my Honors Chemistry classroom feeling inadequate. Our lecture class and laboratory merged so it was very spacious. The teacher, Ms. Staszek sounded as if she was rapping Twista lyrics whenever she spoke.

"Today we're setting up for our last semester project. We'll be making batteries that clean silverware. Some of the things we know we're going to need includes a battery, bakingsoda and..." the teacher rambled on as each letter of her words raced out of her mouth. I found it extremely difficult to keep up. My peers, on the other hand, were all in. They seemed accustomed to her speaking skills. The students held side conversations that showed their understanding of the knowledge. The teacher wrapped up her lecture and exited the room.

"What did she just say?" I asked a kid next to me.

"We have a science project. For now, just bring in an old battery," the kid explained.

I watched one of the White boys get excited. One of them told stories of how he almost burnt his parents' house down. I stuck around after class to get a better understanding of the project. I had the slightest idea as to even what type of battery to bring in. Triple A? Double A? A car battery? Other kids hung around, too. I waited for Ms. Staszek to wrap up an engaged conversation she held with a group of the students. I changed my mind and left the class after hearing the kids and teacher joke about how stupid someone must have been to not know that acetone was flammable. I knew that fact about acetone. Still, I figured the battery question was much more "senseless".

My third-grade pride wouldn't let me stick around. That day, I had a flashback of the incident with Ms. Macklin. I didn't want to be bothered with playing catch up to this new middle-class institution. I worried it'll come with backlash and determined it wasn't worthwhile. By the end of the week, braniacs were already bringing in their batteries and models they completed themselves. I was more confused on what was going on. I slowly changed my seat to one closer to the door. After attendance, I was out.

We had off-campus lunch, so it was easy to get in and out the building. Most Allante and I were the oldest siblings at home by then. My older siblings had already moved out into their own apartments. Pre-calculus and one other class were the only classes I had left to attend after lunch.

Three months in the little country town, and my mama wanted to talk to me about moving back to Chicago. I assumed my mother got information about my absences from class. In the city, truancy officers showed up at doors after the third unexcused absence. More ready to arrest the parent than figure out the status of the absent child. I was relieved when I learned what my mama wanted to talk about had nothing to do with school.

"Yes, Ma?" I glided down our stair banister.

"Shay, Mama is sick," my mama's voice trembled and her eyes were bloodshot red.

"Huh? What's wrong?" I sat down beside my mama.

"Granny... Auntie Ann just called...they're saying she has to get her legs amputated," my mama said.

"But why?" I cried as my throat began to swell around each syllable.

"They believe she have an aneurism," my mama reported.

Out of the blue, my grandma had gotten sick, and we needed to get back to Chicago immediately. The news shocked me. When I left, my grandma was her healthy self—walking and talking perfectly fine. I wanted so badly to understand what went wrong in the short time I had been gone. My family packed our bags and left for Chicago the same day. We drove straight to the hospital. Auntie Ann met us in the lobby. We got visitor's passes rather quickly and moped to my grandma's room in near silence.

"Is she ok?" I shifted the stillness.

"She was sleeping... she's not talking much." Auntie

Ann reported as we turned the corner of the unit where my grandma's room was located.

I crossed my arms. I felt anxious and cold as we approached Mama's area.

"Only a few of us can go in at a time." Auntie Ann said.

I stepped closer to the curtain to get in first. I went inside Mama's room and stood over her bed quietly. Her head and torso, lolled on the rollaway bed positioned at a 45-degree angle. Her eyes and hands lazed similarly. I reached under the covers and mated my grandma's hand with mine. My grandma opened her eyes. She wasn't able to talk much, she just released a few sounds. I knew she would be ok. I held back my tears when I noticed no sign of a leg print underneath my grandma's bed sheet, towards the foot of her bed. I figured my grandma was in pain and didn't want it to show. She always maintained her strength.

My grandma passed away shortly after we made it back to Minnesota from visiting her in the hospital. It was a tough reality to navigate. We returned home, to put her to rest. Chicago felt so empty to me. I didn't want to stay long. When I got back to Minnesota, I didn't want to be there either. I felt alone no matter where I was or what I did.

In Minnesota, we lived far out in the country. Allante and I rode our bikes into town daily, sometimes two or three times a day. There weas not much of a difference in the twenty-minute rides in terms of the desolation of Austin. Just that, in the town there were a few stores, restaurants, and schools. Therefore, it also had the jobs. I worked at a daycare center and McDonalds while Allante worked at an arena. We had just completed our sophomore year of high school. My mother didn't have a car at the time. To make matters even less convenient, public transportations stopped running at five in the evening. It was the worst place to live when you come from a big city like Chicago. It was difficult to adapt. We made it through the summer, but when school started back, our work hours were cut short. I actually had to leave the day care center, the job I loved most.

Allante rode our bikes through the crunchy Fall leaves, into town one Saturday afternoon.

"I'm over this damn place." I said to Man Man. We rested at the bottom of the bridge before we cycled up the steep hill that loved to test our grit. It left us gasping for air each time.

"Me too, I'm thinking about moving back to Chicago," he said.

"For real?" I asked surprisingly "When?"

"Man I don't know but I can't keep doing this," my brother admitted.

"Where you gone stay if you move back?" I inquired.

"I haven't decided, I talked to Uncle Phil. He gave me the ok to come to his place." He said.

Uncle Phil was one of my dad's brothers. He had a football team of kids himself. But he always kept in touch with my brother and I and came through when we needed him, after my dad passed.

"He got a decent size house but idk, he got a big family too," I included.

"Well it will be better than being here," I reckoned.

"If it doesn't work we'll figure something else out, but I gotta get out of this town before it drive me crazy." Allante concluded.

TWO WEEKS LATER, Allante and I left my mama's place in Minnesota. We got on the Grey Hound Bus back to Chicago. We moved in with Uncle Phil.

CHAPTER SEVEN

STREETS OF REALITY

BACK AT TEAM ENGLEWOOD. PATRICE WAS THE MOST excited to see me back. She came to my third period class and requested that I be excused. Our faces lit up when we saw each other.

"You really back!" Patrice blurted.

"Shhh, let's go to the bathroom." I suggested.

We went to the gym instead when we saw the security guard hovering the bathroom area.

"Give me a hug!" I said the minute we walked into the gymnasium. I went to wrap my arms around my friend and felt a baby bump.

"Oh my gosh! When were you going to tell me!!"

"Uhnuhn, I could hurt you right now. Don't ever do that again. You just upped and left me."

"Girl, that's a long story. Can we please talk about it later?"

"Yea, but don't think I'm gone forget because I'm not."

"What's in the oven?" I asked as I rubbed her big ol' belly.

"We're having a baby boy." Patrice was excited and I was just as happy for her. She had been with her high school sweetheart since before I met her. While she wasn't sure she was ready, she was positive things would turn out for the best.

"When are you due?" I asked, "It look like any day, big mama," I laughed.

"December, and girl I know. It feels like it too." Trice added.

"Does Trevell know?" I joked.

Patrice laughed, "Yea, he knows." Patrice rolled her eyes.

"His birthday is in December, too. That fool had the nerve to say if I have my baby on his birthday then I should name it after him." She added.

"Girl, boys say anything out their mouth. But you know he's crazy about you." I reminded her. Trevell had more than a crush on Patrice. He admired her, but he knew she couldn't take him serious. For one, he was too flirty. Besides, Patrice had a boyfriend and way more than that by then. I missed her so much; I started to stay at her family's house many days and nights. We had a lot to get caught up on.

I remember lounging around the house and politicking with family. Khalia and Patrice are blew my phone up for me to hang outside with them.

By the third time they called, Khalia and Patrice had met up with some other friends.

"Y'all oughta meet me at my house then," I requested of them.

"Girl, we just sitting on the porch right now," Khalia said.

"We can come get you when we go to the store though," she added.

"Naw chick, we coming now, and you better be ready--" Patrice interrupted from the background. She knew how I liked to linger.

They lived just a few blocks over, a five-minute walk. Two minutes later they called again to make sure I was dressed.

"Yea?"

"We on our way."

"Cool, I'm ready."

After about twenty minutes and no call, I called Khalia's phone. She didn't answer for me. I felt like they were sending me off and that they hadn't even left to meet me yet. Five minutes later, Khalia called me back.

"Y'all some send-offs. It don't take that long," I said. She said something back that I couldn't make out. Her background noise was too loud. I hung up and called back. She wasn't answering again. One more time then I'm calling it one, I thought.

A crying voice echoed in the phone line.

"Patrice just got shot, g!"

"Who? What? Wait... where y'all at?" I went into a brief array of panicking questions.

Just as she was about to answer. I could already hear sirens and commotion.

Everything around me became a blur. I sprinted out the house and could see nothing but ambulance and police lights at the corner of my block. And red tape as I got closer.

I couldn't cry. I couldn't believe my eyes nor ears. I didn't see anybody I knew. Or maybe I didn't care to. I skimmed the ground inside the perimeter of the tape, and searched for the victim. I didn't see my friend. I only saw blood on the street pavement. Red tape was never a good sign. I stopped to ask somebody what had happened, still in disbelief. It was like there was a million people talking. Bystanders yelled out information. Only thing I caught was that a 16-year-old girl had just got killed. She was shot in the head, others confirmed. My heart dropped, and my body stiffened. I sat on the curb and tears crept down my cheeks easily. I remember feeling like I was awake in a dream.

One of the officers who knew our faces from around the neighborhood was on the scene. He recognized me and came over.

"She's gonna be ok they're taking her to Christ hospital. Her family is heading there now," he attempted to assure me.

I barely felt relief and couldn't reply. He rubbed my shoulder and walked off. All I could think about was Patrice's son. She had just had her baby boy a few months ago. Too often, even authorities, release false information. I needed to know the truth of the matter. I walked over to Patrice family's house in search of clarification. I learned the bullet actually penetrated through her neck. She was taken to the Christ hospital in critical condition. Christ hospital was the nearest trauma center, located in Oaklawn, IL. I worried about my friend's well-being.

This changed our lives forever, taking away my best friend's mobility. I went further into a state of depression but couldn't talk to anybody about it because the only person I really shared my emotions with, was the person who needed me more than ever. I found different ways to mask the pain.

Patrice's incident was only the peak of traumas that hit home base for me. Prior to, I had lost over ten peers I grew up with. After her, at least another ten. No exaggeration. The more people I lost, the more I wanted to be in the neighborhood. I felt like I could influence different possibilities. While often I did, I couldn't cease death from occurring.

———

Dro City Bound

———

DING! "NEXT STOP, 64TH STREET," announced the bus operator over intercom.

I stepped off the Number 4 Cottage Grove bus into a bright sunny day. People posted up on every corner. Wineheads and fiends intermixed on one side of the street. Hustlers hung out on another and youngsters lingered throughout the hood. Some of us infused base in our voices to gain access and demand respect in dice games hoping for a come up. Others, still, found joy in more simple things like chasing the ice cream truck down the block and dangling on the back for a ride to the next corner or two over. That was not all to do in the hood, but that's the gist of it. There's basketball games, pitching, racing, joke sessions, storytelling, you name it. Regardless of our choice of activity, hanging out on the block was our rehab. It's where we ran to figure things out.

I started hustling and lost focus in school, only showing up to ditch depression. Really just scrabbling my priorities. While the talent shows and poetry slams made me feel alive at school, it didn't overpower feeling like the last of a dying breed, literally. My closest peers were vanishing. Yet, I still felt obligated to maintain my reputation at a time disrespecting the dead was at an all-time high. My loyalty and pride wouldn't stand to allow a living being to throw dirt on the name of somebody I grew with, knowing they couldn't defend themselves. Chiraq Art of War, so to say.

I found myself running into more hurdles than I could jump. I couldn't stand to be the icing to my mother's not so crème-filled cake though.

Early in my junior year of high school, I moved out of my mama's place, was barely getting by in school, worked a nine to five that only kept me fed and driven, and made a living off 2 for 15's.

The dime specials kept me well-groomed and apart from the noticeably less fortunate, who were no different from me in the sense surviving took precedence in their lives. My definition of surviving was just a bit more in-depth. I wanted more than to get by. And I needed to look up-kept while doing so.

In essence, we were all kids who lacked the financial and mental resources necessary for finding humane value in the jungle. This lack of stability takes a toll in many ways, but still, we thug it out.

Though product dealing can be a lucrative business with proper discipline, it's accompanied by activities unprofitable. I was fortunate enough to bare the minimum. For my kind of people, young Black kids without proper guidance, that was rewarding enough. Because if you last long enough, you realize there are no real accolades in the streets of reality.

CHAPTER EIGHT

TOGETHER EVERYONE ACHIEVES MORE

A FEW MONTHS AFTER PATRICE'S INCIDENT, JANUARY 8, 2011, I wake up to over fifty missed calls from my close childhood friend, De'Sean and Khalia combined. De' Sean and I went to school together in the suburbs, when we were younger. There we learned we were from the same neighborhood and the rest is history. E, laughed, we fought, we made money together, and we came through for one another. I knew him like the back of my hand. When he called, I felt like something was not right. My stomach had that bubbly feeling. That usually only happened to me when someone died. I didn't know who to call back first but figured De'Sean would be best. We had just hung out the day before.

After the fifth ring, he answered.

"Yea, man," De'Sean said with an abnormally raspy tone.

"What's wrong?" I asked unsure if I really wanted to know.

"Folks dead, g." He cried.

"They bogish man, they bogish," he carried on.

We've had to attend many funerals together. I've even stood by De'Sean on more than one occasion when he's been shot and wounded. But I had never heard him cry before that day. I was scared to ask who died, so I let him have his moment. It didn't take long for him to reveal to me that it was Trevell who had been killed. I went into shock and hung up the phone without a word.

De'Sean lived in the suburbs, so I hoped there was a chance he received some type of misleading information. When we disconnected, I tried to let the news marinate but in that moment, everything felt surreal. I called Khalia.

"Yea, you called?" I asked when she answered on the first ring. I tried to sound calm as if it would alter the reality of things.

"That's crazy Trevell got killed man. You good?" Kay Kay got straight to the point.

My heart stopped.

"Please, say it's not true," I begged of her.

"Ion know but I got a call about it earlier this morning and people putting it on Facebook," Khalia reported.

"Come on. GIVE ME A BREAK!" I cried.

I couldn't hold back the tears anymore. That was the last person on my mind. Trevell had always been so laid back and had so much potential. He was the jokester out the squad, played basketball and was on his way to college.

HIGH SCHOOL at TEAM was redemptive though. Our teachers and staff were utterly real. I like to think they kept everyone afloat. I say this, partly to say everyone grew to know about City's social rapport with girls just as everyone knew of the kids who were too far behind academically to be clowning somebody because their shoes exceeded its life expectancy. Our teachers didn't quite make fun of anyone's imperfections. They simply paid everyone the attention they required and told it like it was. The "stuff" high school students were naïve about. But it went beyond that, when it came to grievance support.

When Trevell passed away, not only did it affect our community, but many students at school as well. Our teachers were very empathetic and supportive during this time. The school made accessible therapists for us to deal with the grief and granted us time to process the loss of our friend. The next home game, they went as far as allowing outsiders come to watch. Previously, the school barred outsiders from attending our school games. With all the fights breaking out in the area, that was the school's way of keeping us safe. Also, a school shooting that left five people injured, at another high school basketball game a few months back, prompted the visitors' restrictions.

In honor of Trevell, they lifted the "no outside guest" policy. A seat was reserved with his jersey, as he would have played in that game. Our school won the basketball game and his mother, and other family and friends from the hood, was able to celebrate his legacy in a positive light.

Although, our teachers were very understanding and compassionate, nothing was peaches and cream. When I would allow my teenage impulses to overrule my ambition to learn, Miss Rushek had absolutely no problem telling me about myself. Ms. Rushek, the generally affable, White woman who taught us English for three years, used to treat me with tough love and dignity. On occasions I thought I needed to go back and forth with her as if I had some logical point to prove, she didn't mind putting me out of her classroom either. The minute I was ready to be positively active, I had complete access to reenter and join in. To be certain, my head was on right, Miss Rushek would call on me to participate. She was this way with everyone.

Ms. Flowers looped with us as well. She was a plump Black woman who had a new hairstyle every Monday morning. She didn't put up with our shit. Allante and I had her the same period our junior year. Match us two with James, Dushan, and Avery. James was the straight up fashionable hood boy with intellect. Dushan was the mellow guy, maybe 4 ft. 10, and the furthest from wimpy. Avery was the pretty boy demeanor, wavy dude. They were all cool kids, witty, and slick as oil. Hustlers too. The five of us would race to finish our assignments just to crack jokes until we were uncontrollably tickled. Either that or get a quick dice game going. Ms. Flowers couldn't care less how smart any one of us were when it came to disturbing the rest of her students. Not that they weren't part of the entertainment, too. She was just well aware of the fact not everybody could afford to joke around. For that reason, Ms. Flowers was adamant about granting every one of us equal opportunities to complete our work.

One day, she sat at her desk in such a calm and virtuous manner, as usual. She warned us repeatedly to gain self-control. We were laughing hysterically. It was probably about something Dushan had said. His jokes and the way he delivered them was always the funniest. Dushan had a tendency to be so smooth and would say things we would least expect him to say.

Avery laughed obnoxiously at whatever the joke may have been. His laugh triggered the rest of us.

"Dude your ass laughing like you sick," James teased Avery.

"Aw bro now I'm about to flame you," Avery defended himself as the other three of us contributed with giggles.

"Alright, I've asked y'all to settle down. Avery, James, Ashante and Allante get out of my classroom. We were pissed when Dushan wasn't excused but we went to run the hallways.

James and I clicked from the start, and I had a tighter bond with him than the other guys. He considered me to be his lil' sister. We had more in common than school. We both found fulfillment in money and city lights just as much as we found it in being enlightened. I started hanging out with him on his side of town.

———

Moving on Up

———

THE SOUTH SIDE of Chicago was becoming a lot like a Call of Duty battleground. What should've been my last straw, in my neck of the woods, was the moment I found myself eye to eye with the barrel of a handgun.

Willisha and I lingered on the corner of 66th and Drexel exchanging laughs with a crowd of locals when we saw De'Sean and his guys walk up. Willisha and I had been close friends for two years. I knew her since I was younger, her family and my family had been around each other for as long as either of us can remember.

"Y'all going to Ellis Park?" Willlisha directed her question to the group, no one in particular.

"Hell naw, we just came from that way. We just marching through the hood." De'Sean responded.

"Is it people out there?" Willisha asked

"Yea its a few— yoooo!" De'Sean was distracted as a champagne colored car rolled up alongside us on 66th St. Inside the car was a group of guys twisting their fingers. The sun had gone down already so visibility was restricted. Just as De'Sean went to reciprocate the gestures, the front and back seat passengers raised guns up and out the windows in near unison. My heart paused as I watched kids left to fend for themselves when their young mothers turned them loose to run for safety.

"Clear this muhfuckin' block, before we clear it," one of the passengers demanded for us to relocate. The car peeled out after the pistol-toter warned us to clear the block. It had to have been the occupied baby stroller left without an attendant that kept him from ringing the alarm right then.

We tried calling our friends a couple blocks over to warn them after seeing the direction the vehicle headed. It was too late. Three familiar faces had been shot. Fortunately, they were in stable condition.

In instances like these, we count our blessings and keep it moving.

Abnormal

I WAS MORE INFATUATED with the grind than shootouts. So, even though I didn't dismiss the hood altogether, I laid off for a bit. I swapped out days in the trap for late nights in Lamron. The heart of Lamron, a Chicago neighborhood, was just two blocks over from TEAM Englewood high school. It stretched a couple blocks in each direction. This is where James was from. I started linking up with him after school. I earned my respect in Jame's hood, pretty much how I did everywhere else- keeping my money and morals in check. Although Lamron wasn't any more of a peace zone than Dro City, there was more structure. I needed that. After school, instead of an almost sure game of "Point Em' Out Call Em' Out", I opted to shoot dice with the Barksdales. I striked more often than not, playing seven-eleven on Normal. I tribute much of my winnings to dudes that got anxious when they saw a female on a come-up.

On my first day, I was welcomed with an invitation to "score".

"Get down, mf!" Rob challenged James.

"Get down, mf," James mocked, "you know I'm with it. You see I got Missy with me too, let's get it kid!"

Rob laughed at James, "I'm about to strike you and her boi."

I laughed. The three of us hit the gangway and ticked up for seven eleven. Soon after, some more of their guys joined us. Dice rolling was accompanied by shit talking. Mostly, from the roller or the fader. Then you had your color commentators, too.

"Oou, take her ass down," somebody yelled out as he turned the corner and peeped me reach downward for the dice.

I wasn't the first girl they seen shoot dice. It still tended to surprise the dude to see a fresh lady-face get down with the fellas. I had the audacity to be doing so in a hood outside of my own. James backed off when he threw a few craps in a row. I was up against three of his homies. Two hours in and two of the other dudes chipped away. That resulted in a toe-to-toe with Lil Rob and me betting back and forth. James friend, Lil Rob was relentless on the dice. Just when I came close to taking him all the way down, he convinced me to give him a 6/8 bet on my roll. For the next five rolls, it was two, three, twelve, when the dice stopped. I let him shoot his shot once more, and then I called it quits while I was still up a decent amount. I felt like I had an advantage of beginner's luck in their hood. I went back the next day. And days after that. I was on a winning spree for a few days. Either winning something or going up then breaking even.

I found myself on Normal on a Thursday night. I sprinted after dollars that had too much of a head start. It wasn't my intentions to partake in the marathon, but I was already in the race, when one of Lamron's old heads pulled up. We had been squatting and bending for close to three hours already- for what the old head considered petty bucks. He pulled out his bankroll and challenged Lil Rob to up the pot.

"Forty I go, forty I hit." The old head declared.

His bankroll was big enough to feed the projects. I was up enough for my hunger to be already satisfied. The idea of more made my stomach growl. After a few throws focused strictly on his fader, the big homie threw a bet in the air. I jumped on it and he crapped out. Of course big mills were suited for an even bigger mouth. The old head humbugged more than all other participants combined.

"Shit! I knew not to bet you. I'm on your ass now lil lady," he announced. I held my poker face without replying. I knew I had opened the door to be the dude target. I continued to make bets with him and ended up irritated and sidetracked by all of the bluffing. A lesson I should've already learned from playing with my blood brothers. I left the game with a hundred dollars after being up nearly two thousand. Talk about a punch in the gut. I hung around their block for a bit longer. Soon enough another "petty" dice game had struck. It was well after 1 a.m., and there I was scrabbling for a few measly bucks. I had been hanging around for some weeks then and felt comfortable. The guys in Lamron showed me love and talked their talk equally. Same way they did with each other.

It wasn't long before people started to scatter. My phone screened lit up at 2:27a.m. I had a decent stash tucked in my right jacket pocket. I continued to tuck a few bucks every other point I hit. It winded down to me and another one of their guys. I wasn't very familiar with him. I saw him hanging around the block before but he had never played dice with us. He usually just observed. His aura was magnetic.

"You must be up Missy, you got my boy involved." James approached.

"Naw, I'm tryna get back man." I replied to James.

Everyone else stayed around and watched as the kicked it. We went toe-to-toe before I found myself peeling from my jacket pocket. The dude wiped me out then counted the money in my face. He reached to hand me some of it back.

"I'm good," I said coolly.

I was salty I took a "L" for the second time in one night. I did not need his pity though. I had been playing the game since roughly eight. I knew what my chances were as well as what came with it.

He laughed at me nonchalantly. "Here, girl."

Sensing his genuine energy early on, I crossed my arm to rest my elbow as I bent a forearm and extended my hand.

"What's your name?" he asked as handed me the cash.

"Missy. What's yours and why you being so easy on me?"

"Cus I just took yo' ass down." His chuckle swayed with intent.

"You got lucky, you don't even shoot dice!" I snapped at him.

"Yea, aight. Don't ever underestimate a person."

He laughed again as he walked out the park.

I followed behind him, with a slight skip to keep up with his long legs and big steps.

"Wait, I never got your name."

"You don't forget nun'n do you Missy?"

"You ain't the only person aware out here."

"You funny" he smiled. "B."

"Don't call me no B when its gangsta running in my veins," I joked.

I had him tickled at that point.

"Gangsta, huh? Your ass crazy."

He hopped up on the stomp of one of the houses on the block. "That's my name, girl."

"Oh."

I walked up the steps and sat beside him, uninvited.

"What make you figure I underestimated you tho?"

"You didn't expect me to take your bread did you?"

"Yea, you right but that's cause..."

"Yea, yea."

That was the first thing he had taught me, unknowingly. We actually had more in common than I would've guessed. We talked for a few more minutes and watched the block start to get empty as people scattered. The sun started to rise from the east and birds began chirping.

I had to be at school in two hours. We walked towards 63rd and parted ways. I had been awake all night but felt awakened by this interaction. Something inside me sparked.

I no longer went on Normal, solely for dice games. I

sensed more. A few days in a row, I walked through there in search of B. He was ghost. I ran into him the night of our homecoming, and he remembered who I was. He nodded his head, "What's up, kid?"

A smile was written lightly across my face as I approached the church steps.

"Can I sit here?" I asked.

"Gone head."

I plugged my ears with my headphones and sat two steps above him. I mimicked him as he observed the continuous traffic of the block. People walking thru and cars riding by. Every once in a while, B dropped a few jewels on me. The importance of loving some people from a distance was a major one. One that he didn't speak verbally. Instead, I took notice. He connected to everything around him. And attached to nothing. The more I hung around him, the more ambivalent I became about my place in the world. I decided I would get away after high school. My plan was to hustle hard, save my money, and move my family away. Of all the money I made on Normal, I took most pride in the morals I had to value when I parted ways with the block. I won a dear friend who never had to be around me for to feel his presence. More importantly, the outer world didn't bound B. I always felt that no matter the lack of resources made available to me, that I was not limited. Meeting B, served as a reminder. It was time to act on my imaginations of moving on up.

CHAPTER NINE

LOVE LIBERATES

Where do we go from here? Senior year, I started gravitating towards vulnerability. I hung out with Sonsi more. Sonsi was the prettiest girl in the school that nearly everybody had the wrong perception of. She was the girl not many people took the time to get to know. The cool boys flirted with her pridefully, while the guys with low self-esteem steered clear of her because she had a high maintenance presentation. Before we started hanging out, I didn't pay her much attention. When we first talked, I noticed a piece of myself in her. It felt like a piece of myself that I had not came to terms with, just yet. Her grace and gratitude in any situation, spoke to me in a way that I knew we were meant to be in each other's life. Still I didn't know how to expose that poise just yet. I always felt like I had to defend myself from something.

At 8 a.m, I was dismissed from class. Thirty minutes ago, Mr. Zimmerman stood at the desk with a yellow write up in his hand. We gathered outside of the classroom.

When the bell rang, we made our way to our desks. Before I could take out my notebook, the intercom had come on. Announcements normally don't come on until five minutes into class. Mr. Z posted up on the wall under the speaker, waiting for an answer that never came through from the dean's office.

"I'm going to make copies of today's assignment," he announced to the class, with a face of discernment dipped in culpability.

He came back with a stack of papers blocking his face and a security guard trailing behind him.

Mr. Z exchanged the stack of papers for the referral sitting on his desk. I made eye contact with the teacher and security through the spaces of student limbs. Officer Wilson, the security guard, signaled for me.

Slightly confused, I didn't budge.

"All right now, settle down," Mr. Z addressed the class.

"Let's go Ms. Gills. Security is here for you."

"Dang, what you do now?" Dushan asked.

I smacked my lips. "I ain't do nothing and I ain't going nowhere."

"He hate you," James student added.

"Tell me about it." I sighed.

"Man don't go," somebody else whispered.

"Just go, nothing's gone happen. He bullshittin'," James commented.

"It's too early for your shit," Kiwi snapped at me rolling his eyes.

Kiwi, was pretty gay boy who hung out with Sonseriya. Therefore, we were mutually cool. He was straightforward about just about everything.

My peers commentating only made it worst though. At that point, I didn't care.

"Fuck you, Kiwi. As a matter of fact, maybe you can explain this cus I'm certain I ain't done nothing worthy of being escorted out of class for, this early"

"Girlllll," Kiwi rebutted leery of my attitude.

"It's ok. You don't have to respond to none them. He is wrong for that cause class just started, but just go ahead and explain everything to Ms. Korellis," Sonseriya prompted me. I was reluctant but I knew she was right.

The security guard threw his hands up and left. The door closed behind him

Not even three minutes later, Ms. Korellis face appeared theough the glass window of the classroom door. When I saw her, I gathered my things to leave. I had a different type of respect for her. No matter how right I thought I was, if she said something, I knew it to be harmless. I trailed her to her sanctuary. I watched the reflection of pain through Ms. Korellis eyes. As I sat in her office, anger did not echoe. Agony rather, bounced off the walls. Air-conditioned, cold layers began to peel back from my arms. At the sound of the bell, Ms. Korellis stood up to grant us privacy. Her long floral dress settled on the floor, complimenting her distressed vibration. After a few minutes of silence, we had a heart to heart. I felt refreshed with a reminder that I wanted more for myself. I was still troubled by some things though. I sat in silence, marinating in bother. I never figured out why I had been wrote-up in the first place, just that the nature of the issue was meaningless.

There was so much anger built up that wasn't allowed to be expressed. I found myself laughing when nothing was funny. Crying when I should have been speaking. And silent when I preferred to be crying. We become comfortable with reacting in situations we're not taught how to respond to. Chats with Ms. Korellis served as a segue to evolution, for me. The allowing to articulate feelings was revival and the beginning of unraveling distorted views.

A few days later, during first period, Marine recruiters came to speak with the 2012 graduating class. He spoke about the awesome benefits of joining the military. I was captured by the thought of free school and travel. No one in my family had ever graduated college. In fact, many people I knew had not obtained a high school diploma. The success stories I heard were bitter sweet. They included people that graduated with a degree that they had to spend most of their "working" years paying back. I was ambitious but not stupid. I wanted to exceed but the idea of 40k worth of debt never captured me. Not surprising, Allante and Dushan thought just as I did. When the bell rang, most of our class-mates were happy to be relieved. The three of us stuck around and gave the recruiter our information. The recruiter kept in contact for a while. When we graduated, he took us to take the practice ASVAB. We all got passing scores and scheduled to come out and train with the recruiters during the week. We discussed that our recruiter was to pick us up twice a week. Soon after, we never heard from the recruiter person again.

I began receiving acceptance letters from schools. Allanté and I learned that we had scored the highest of our graduating class on the ACT test. The ACT is used to assess your competency and generally, is one way to obtain scholarships to schools. We began submitting college applications and two to three weeks later acceptance letters were rolling in. Of the many I received, Philander Univer-sity in Arkansas had my interest most. They offered me a full tuition scholarship. I considered them over the other options mostly because my big sister was accepted to UAPB the year prior. She took them up on their offer and moved to Arkansas. I wanted to be closer to my sister when I graduated high school.

I was fortunate to visit the school and partook in student campus life for the first time. It was just as fun as I imagined. Then my dreams of attending Philander began to fade to dust when I got news that my sister apartment was broken into out in Pine Bluff. She was ready to return home and I changed my mind about leaving. Instead, I attended University of Illinois at Chicago and stayed home.

Third District

SCREECHING tires out spoke the Pandora commercial vibes in my ears. I leaped backwards as a squad car hit the alley, interfering my stroll. My earphones were stuck on my zipper as I jerked my neck from twelve o'clock to six, startled by the cop cars swarming the block. The driving officer of the first vehicle pumped his breaks and blocked the crossing. My bag of Hot Krunchy Kurl chips hit the pavement as the jakes jumped out of their cars in a rage. There were four male officers in one squad car. They jumped out with nothing short of poker faces on display. Two of them, locked and loaded when their boots hit the ground. They broke from the back seat before the wheels stopped rolling. Their doors left open. I pushed myself up against the building of Meme's African braiding shop when one of the officers brushed up against me. His attention was on his colleagues and his talkie as he called in the direction a suspect must've fled to the dispatch. They were on a foot chase.

Once they passed by, I kept it moving towards Ellis park. My phone vibrated inside my khaki pants by the time I made it to Drexel, two block west of Ellis. I was startled as a squad car raced up the one way before I could retrieve the phone from my pocket. Four more cars came from opposing directions. One was on the tail of a 2000 Lincoln when it hit the curb and loss control of its steering wheel two blocks over. I sped up my pace and settled on the first familiar porch. I recovered my phone in time to catch it ringing again. An unknown contact displayed on my Galaxy screen. I was about to ignore the call but something urged me to answer.

"Hello?"

"Ashanté!"

"Hey, why are you-"

"Look, I need you to do something." The male voice came to a calm.

"I need you to go pick up a pistol and meet these detectives"

"What the fuck? Are you ser—" the phone clicked.

As terrified as I was, I had heard many stories from people I knew personally who had been in similar situations with the cops. In these instances, detectives offered young boys their freedom in exchange for a firearm. Often times, if the boys had nothing to give, they faced more extensive charges than the "crime" committed. I tried to think of other ways to get the pistol to the detective without being involved, but with no way of calling the jail back, I was clueless. I felt obliged by loyalty and the demand to assist someone to escape such madness and corruption. I tied my ACG Nike boots, said a prayer, and executed the plan. I power-walked back west towards Cottage Grove. The streetlights seemed to have followed me every step of the way as if I were performing on Broadway. I turned into a familiar neighborhood alley and wiggled my hand under the identified garage door that wouldn't lift no higher than the intended crack. The tight squeeze left a skin scrape on the back of my hand. I stood at the end of the alley, with a pistol inside a brown paper bag that I had found in the vacant garage, until I saw the squad car pull through. They stopped midway. My heart felt like there were drummers up against my arteries, as I watched them for two minutes before making myself visible. The wheels began to roll slowly and the car was so quiet I couldn't tell the engine was on. The Hispanic driver looked me in my eyes as he continued driving towards me. I looked away, uncertain if these were the right cops.

He nodded his head, to signal my cooperation.

I made it thru hell and high waters.

I forgot to lick the good ol' vitners seasoning off my fingers.

I thought about the scholarship to Philander. I wondered if it was too late to take them up on their offer. At this point all I know is this place isn't for me. I regretted not taking the scholarship to Philander Smith College. I contemplated a new way for hours. I was happy when I learned that I helped. From a felony conspiracy charge to a misdemeanor possession—I felt uneasy, knowing that someone's life was gambled at the leisure of another person. I wanted to change my environment. I decided that I was going to join the Army.

July 24, 2013, two days after my birthday, I swore in and received my departure date. The other eleven kids were excited and that made me more excited. I waited for a feeling of relief to come by, but it never showed. I drove back to my neighborhood, and continued my normal life. Eventually, sharing the news with my family. They didn't take me serious. I had three months before I was to fly out to South Carolina for Basic Combat Training. I never spoke about leaving again. When the day came, I rejoiced.

EPILOGUE

Prior to writing, I never spoke of how devastated I felt regarding Patrice's situation. Of all devastations, this weighed on me most. I couldn't understand how a soul as beautiful as hers can be deserving of something so brutal. Still, she has helped me cope and understand reality more.

Watching Patrice channel her trauma over the years had relieved me in a way that no amount of counseling could have ever. Seeing how she didn't dwell on what should be. As much as she wants to be more active in the world and in her son's life, she does not let the idea dictate her happiness. A true warrior, in my eyes.

I see the joy and peace she has and know that it is a direct result of her love for life. I have learned to laugh more, live freely, and grow through any and all obstacles in the same manner. There is freedom in focusing more on the things you love and prioritizing the things that truly matter most. Family matters most.

. . .

I TOOK a trip to California earlier this year and spent most of my days at Lake Merritt out in Oakland. I knew absolutely no one in the area except for my aunt and cousin who were within a 20-mile radius. I checked in with them once or twice but preferred to be in my own space. My family worried about me. They called and texted every single day.

It wasn't long before strangers started gravitating towards me. Here at Lake Merritt, I met some of the most genuine people I could have ever imagined.

I have never felt so liberated in my life. The water, the birds, the geese, the musicians, the undisturbed naps. It was all so calming. Every morning I sat out on the grass, reading, writing, and doing yoga. It felt as if I was in a different world.

Spending time around those that loved with no reasoning kept me grounded. My passion for creating art developed and enhanced. I have learned to grow and become comfortable with being uncomfortable. Spending time out in nature, preferably near water, keeps me present. I love to meditate, journal and write poetry near the water.

To be in a place where the homeless rates are crazy high and see so much civilization often brought tears to my eyes. I can't help but be gracious. Feeling divinely annihilated, I thanked God as I inhaled life and exhaled my fears.

It was at Lake Merritt where this book came through me. Jay-Z once wrote something like, "Sometimes what we need most is to hear our story told back to us." That spoke volumes to me. And it's the most virtuous statement I've ever heard, from one legend to another. That's where I get an understanding of myself from and where I'm able to grant my peers an understanding of life. It's where sanity lies.

It is important to be both mindful and mindless. Being

mindful is understanding that you are entitled to your emotions. Being mindless is letting it go. I will never forget where I come from, the challenges I have overcome, nor will I mistake it for who I am. If you forget these things, then it's likely you'll forget the lessons they brought forth. Life is like a puzzle; every piece plays its part in making us whole.

After spending a few months at Lake Merritt, I returned home to my family feeling regal and more influential. I have come to realize that I have survived a thousand deaths already. They've only alleviated my fears.

SO, where do we go from here? We go inside. We live.

ACKNOWLEDGMENTS

My definition of relentless. My example of a hustler. Thank you for your unconditional love and all you have sacrificed for the health and well-being of your family. I love you Ma.

Here is to a woman. A woman that is colorblind. A selfless woman of love. A woman of integrity. A woman I hold dear to my heart. Peggy Korellis, thank you.

Kelli Rushek, thank you for such warm welcomes into a new passion. I appreciate all of your insight. I am floored by your generosity.

The readers, I'm honored to speak intimately with each and every one of you.

My brother's and sisters from the hood, We Are One.

Thank you for your listening ear and open heart.

TEAM ENGLEWOOD

There is not enough words for me to express my gratitude for the foundation built at TEAM. As I reflect on life, more now than ever, TEAM plays a big part in my personal growth and development. TEAM served as a home away from home. So many good memories, I can't choose one. I admire how many of our teachers took the Red Line. Even if they didn't know the specifics, they were able to get a glimpse of what was going on in the community. Our security guards were committed to their roles and stood frontline whenever necessary. It saddens me, the school is being closed but I'm happy to say:

Its value cannot be diminished.

Made in the USA
Columbia, SC
14 March 2019